AF527479

MAHA KUMBH: A SCIENTIFIC TREASURE TROVE

(Maha Kumbh a haven for Scientists)

Dr. C S Rayudu

Amazon.com

Copyright © 2025 Dr. C S Rayudu

MAHA KUMBH: A SCIENTIFIC TREASURE TROVE
(Maha Kumbh: A Haven for Scientists)

All rights reserved. No part of this book may be reproduced, distributed, or transmitted in any form or by any means, including photocopying, recording, or other electronic or mechanical methods, without the prior written permission of the author or publisher, except in the case of brief quotations used in critical reviews or scholarly articles as permitted by copyright law.

Disclaimer:

This book, 'Maha Kumbh: A Scientific Treasure Trove,' (Maha Kumbh: A Haven for Scientists) is intended for educational and informational purposes only. The author and publisher have made every effort to ensure the accuracy of the content but disclaim liability for any errors or interpretations.

Dr. C S Rayudu
ISBN: 978-93-342-1314-0
Printed in India

For permission requests, write to:
drcsrayudu@gmail.com

The book, 'Maha Kumbh: A Scientific Treasure Trove' (Maha Kumbh a haven for Scientists) dedicated to my beloved parents, father Shri Cirigire Subbanna and mother Smt. Cirigire Papamma

CONTENTS

PREFACE

The Maha Kumbh, the very name conjures images of a vast, swirling confluence of humanity, a spectacle of vibrant spirituality and ancient tradition. For millennia, pilgrims have journeyed to this sacred gathering, drawn by the promise of purification and spiritual enlightenment. But beneath the surface of ritual and devotion lies another, often overlooked, dimension: a scientific treasure trove waiting to be explored.

This book, "Maha Kumbh: A Scientific Treasure Trove," ventures beyond the well-trodden paths of religious and cultural interpretation to reveal the unique potential the Maha Kumbh holds for scientific inquiry. We argue that this monumental event is far from being solely a spiritual pilgrimage; it presents an unprecedented opportunity to study human behaviour, environmental impact, and the very fabric of our collective consciousness.

Maha Kumbh is a vast living laboratory where millions engage in shared practices, forming an unparalleled real-time experiment. This is precisely what the Maha Kumbh offers. It allows researchers to examine the effects of mass gatherings on local ecosystems, analyse the psychological dynamics of large populations, and delve into the impacts of ancient rituals on physical and mental well-being. It provides data points rarely, if ever, accessible in traditional scientific settings.

This book is not intended to diminish the profound spiritual significance of the Maha Kumbh. Rather, we seek to demonstrate how science and spirituality can coexist and, indeed, enrich one another. By applying rigorous scientific methodologies to the study of this event, we aim to deepen our understanding of the human experience while also highlighting the need for responsible and sustainable practices in mass gatherings.

"Maha Kumbh: A Scientific Treasure Trove" is a call to action for scientists, researchers, and anyone curious about the untapped potential of this extraordinary event. We invite you to embark on a journey that blends the wisdom of the ages with the rigours of modern science, revealing the hidden scientific gems nestled in the heart of the Maha Kumbh. This is more than just an academic pursuit; it is a pathway toward a more holistic understanding of ourselves and our place in the universe. It is time to recognise the Maha Kumbh as not only a haven for the spirit but also a remarkable haven for scientists.

Dr. C S Rayudu

INTRODUCTION

Maha Kumbh: A Scientific Treasure Trove

For millennia, India has been recognised as a hub for profound spiritual seekers, a fount of ancient wisdom, and a fusion of diverse human experiences. At the core of this complex tapestry is the Kumbh Mela, a cyclical gathering of unprecedented proportions. Despite its well-known spiritual importance, the Kumbh, especially the Maha Kumbh hosted in Prayagraj, stands out as something genuinely extraordinary: a lively, dynamic, and extremely fruitful ground for scientific research. This book, "Maha Kumbh: A Scientific Treasure Trove," is committed to revealing the Maha Kumbh's mostly untapped potential, presenting it not just as a spiritual pilgrimage, but also as an unmatched "living laboratory."

Primary Objective to Emphasise

The major goal is to highlight the Maha Kumbh as a unique scientific opportunity, a shelter for not just spiritual seekers but also scientists and researchers from other fields. This happening all at once, especially at Prayagraj, is a very rare "once every three generations" event. It creates a place where the sheer number of people, the intensity of spiritual practice, and the unique natural background make it an unbeatable place to ask questions. Here, traditional knowledge and meditation traditions are enhanced, resulting in a "living library" of human experience ready for scientific analysis.

Hidden Paths and Future Prospects in Scientific Discovery

"Maha Kumbh: A Scientific Treasure Trove" contends that the Kumbh is, at its heart, a hub of scientific inquiry waiting to be fully explored. This book seeks to deconstruct and demystify its possibilities, going beyond the conventional story to show how its distinct ecosystem might provide insights into human behaviour, awareness, environmental repercussions, epidemiological trends, and much more. We will investigate the Maha Kumbh's secrets and prospects for scientific discovery.

Promising Frontiers for Research

This book encourages scholars, researchers, and anyone interested in the interaction of science, spirituality, and large-scale human events to investigate the Maha Kumbh's unique scientific potential. By exploring the philosophical and practical components of this massive meeting, we can see its potential as a focus for experimentation, discovery, and the formation of shared knowledge. From the secrets of the human mind to the logistical skills necessary to manage millions, the Maha Kumbh is a deep and fascinating source of research. The book demonstrates how this unique occurrence might serve as a paradigm for new cooperation between science and spiritual tradition, stretching the limits of our collective knowledge. The book concludes with suggestions for several new scientific directions that expand upon previous research. We could study some intriguing topics further, encompassing a wide range of cultural, spiritual, and practical issues. The studies' findings may suggest potential areas for further study.

CHAPTER 1: THE MAHA KUMBH – MORE THAN A PILGRIMAGE

The Kumbh Mela—a name that resonates with spiritual fervour and evokes images of a sea of humanity converging at the confluence of sacred rivers—is far more than just a pilgrimage. It is a phenomenon that defies simple categorisation—a complex tapestry woven with threads of ancient mythology, historical tradition, profound religious significance, and increasingly intriguing scientific possibilities. This introduction aims to provide a comprehensive overview of the Kumbh Mela and its multifaceted significance, laying the groundwork for a deeper exploration of its scientific potential.

1. A Brief Overview of the Kumbh Mela and Its Significance:

The Kumbh Mela is a mass Hindu pilgrimage, a colossal festival that occurs four times every twelve years, rotating between four sacred locations: Haridwar, Prayagraj (formerly Allahabad), Nashik, and Ujjain. These locations are not chosen arbitrarily; they are all situated at the confluence of sacred rivers, known as *Sangams*, which are believed to possess immense spiritual purifying power. The precise timing of the Mela is determined by complex astrological calculations, based on the positions of Jupiter, the Sun, and the Moon in relation to specific zodiac signs. This celestial alignment is believed to occur at these specific intervals, marking a particularly auspicious time for ritual bathing and the attainment of spiritual liberation, or moksha.

The roots of the Kumbh Mela are deeply intertwined with Hindu mythology, particularly the captivating tale of the *Samudra Manthan*, the churning of the cosmic ocean. This epic narrative describes the joint effort of gods (Devas) and demons (Asuras) to churn the ocean of milk in search of Amrita, the nectar of immortality. During this tumultuous process, several divine objects emerged, including the coveted nectar. As the gods and demons fought over the Amrita, a few drops are believed to have spilt onto the earth at the four locations where the Kumbh Mela is held. These locations, thus sanctified by the touch of divine nectar, became centres of pilgrimage and focal points for the Kumbh Mela. The Mela, therefore, commemorates this mythical event, offering devotees the opportunity to partake in the same divine energy by bathing in the holy waters at the auspicious time.

The Kumbh Mela is not simply about bathing, however. It is a vibrant and dynamic expression of Hindu culture and tradition. It brings together millions of pilgrims from all walks of life, transcending caste, social status, and linguistic barriers. The Mela creates a temporary tent city of unparalleled scale, a sprawling metropolis that pulsates with life, devotion, and a shared sense of purpose. Within this ephemeral city, one finds a microcosm of India itself, a kaleidoscope of diverse languages, customs, and spiritual practices coexisting in a remarkable harmony. The Kumbh Mela is a melting pot of religious discourse, with countless saints, gurus, and spiritual leaders holding discourses, leading prayers, and sharing their wisdom. It is a platform for spiritual seekers to engage in religious debates, listen to learned scholars, and deepen their understanding of Hindu philosophy and scripture.

Spectacle of Profound Devotion

The Mela is also a spectacle of profound devotion. One witnesses the unwavering faith of the masses; the vibrant colours of religious attire; the rhythmic chanting of mantras that fill the air; and the deeply moving rituals that have been passed down through generations. The sight of millions of people bathing in the sacred waters, their faces lit up with devotion and hope, is a testament to the enduring power of faith. The Kumbh Mela is a place where one can witness the raw, unfiltered expression of religious fervor—a phenomenon that is both awe-inspiring and humbling.

The sheer scale of the Kumbh Mela is staggering. It is estimated that tens of millions of pilgrims participate in the major bathing days, making it the largest gathering of human beings on the planet. The logistics of managing such a massive crowd are immense, requiring meticulous planning and coordination by government authorities. Providing sanitation, security, and transportation for millions of people is a monumental task, and the successful execution of Kumbh Mela is a testament to the organisational capabilities of the organisers. The Mela is not just a spiritual event; it is a logistical marvel, a demonstration of the ability to manage complexity and ensure order amidst chaos.

Social and Cultural Importance

Beyond the spiritual and logistical aspects, the Kumbh Mela also holds significant social and cultural importance It serves as a platform for cultural exchange, where people from different regions and backgrounds come together, sharing their traditions and customs. The Mela also plays a role in reinforcing social bonds and strengthening community ties. Pilgrims often travel to the Kumbh Mela in groups, fostering a sense of camaraderie and shared experience. The Mela, therefore, is not just an individual journey of faith; it is also a collective experience that strengthens social cohesion.

In recent years, the Kumbh Mela has also attracted the attention of scientists and researchers from various disciplines. The sheer scale of the gathering, the unique environment, and deep-rooted traditions offer researchers an unparalleled opportunity to study a wide range of phenomena, from human behaviour and crowd dynamics to the impact of faith on health and well-being. The Kumbh Mela, therefore, is evolving into a unique laboratory for scientific inquiry, adding another layer of significance to this already multifaceted event. This book will delve deeper into these scientific aspects, exploring the potential for groundbreaking research and the insights that can be gained from studying this extraordinary phenomenon.

2. Book's Objective: Exploring the Scientific Opportunities of the Maha Kumbh

This book embarks on a journey to explore a dimension of the Maha Kumbh that, while often overshadowed by its profound spiritual significance, holds immense potential for scientific discovery: the wealth of opportunities it presents for research across a multitude of disciplines. While acknowledging and respecting the deep-rooted faith and traditions associated with the Kumbh Mela, this book aims to illuminate its potential as a unique, large-scale, and naturally occurring laboratory for scientific inquiry. It proposes that the Maha Kumbh, with its massive population, its unique socio-cultural context, and the sheer scale of the event, offers an unparalleled platform to investigate a wide range of phenomena related to human behaviour, social dynamics, public health, environmental science, and even the very nature of belief and consciousness.

The book's objective is not to diminish or question the spiritual importance of the Kumbh Mela. On the contrary, it seeks to complement our understanding of this extraordinary event by exploring its scientific dimensions. It recognises that spirituality and science are not mutually exclusive; they can coexist and even inform each other. By examining the Maha Kumbh through a scientific lens, we can gain new insights into the human condition, the power of collective experience, and the intricate relationship between mind, body, and spirit. The book posits that scientific inquiry can enhance our appreciation for the complexity and wonder of the Kumbh Mela, revealing layers of understanding beyond its traditional religious interpretations.

The exploration stems from the recognition that the Maha Kumbh, by its very nature, creates a unique environment ripe for scientific investigation. The sheer number of individuals participating in the pilgrimage presents researchers with an unprecedented opportunity to study human behaviour on a massive scale. How do individuals interact within such a large crowd? How are social norms established and maintained in this temporary mega-city? How does collective emotion manifest itself and influence individual behaviour? Researchers can explore these and other related questions through the lens of social psychology and crowd dynamics. The Maha Kumbh allows researchers to observe and analyse these phenomena in a real-world setting, providing valuable data that can be applied to understanding and managing large gatherings in other contexts, such as festivals, sporting events, or even disaster relief efforts.

Public Health

Furthermore, the Kumbh Mela offers a fertile ground for research in the field of public health. The congregation of millions of people from diverse backgrounds, often with varying levels of access to healthcare and sanitation, presents unique challenges for disease control and prevention. Studying the spread of infectious diseases during the Kumbh Mela can provide valuable insights into epidemiology and inform public health strategies for managing large gatherings. Researchers can also investigate the impact of the pilgrimage on the health and well-being of the participants, examining factors such as stress levels, immune function, and the effects of ritualistic practices on physical and mental health. This research can contribute to our understanding of the complex interplay between social, environmental, and individual factors that influence health outcomes.

Environmental Impact

The environmental impact of the Maha Kumbh is another area ripe for scientific investigation. The sheer volume of waste generated by millions of pilgrims, the management of sanitation, and the potential impact on the water quality of the sacred rivers are all critical areas of concern. Environmental scientists can study these issues, developing strategies for minimising the ecological footprint of Mela and ensuring its sustainability. Research in this area can lead to innovative solutions for waste management, water purification, and environmental protection in other large-scale events as well.

Religious Beliefs and Practices

Beyond the more tangible areas of research, the Maha Kumbh also offers a unique opportunity to explore the less tangible aspects of human experience, such as the role of faith and spirituality in human life. Studies have shown that religious beliefs and practices can have a positive impact on physical and mental well-being. The Kumbh Mela, with its intense focus on spiritual practices and collective worship, provides a natural setting to investigate these connections further. Researchers can explore how faith influences health outcomes, how pilgrimage affects psychological well-being, and how collective rituals shape individual identity and sense of belonging. This research can contribute to our understanding of the mind-body connection and the potential benefits of spiritual practices, even if those benefits are understood through a secular, scientific framework.

The book, therefore, aims to be a comprehensive exploration of the scientific opportunities presented by the Maha Kumbh. It will delve into various disciplines, including sociology, psychology, anthropology, medicine, environmental science, and even religious studies, exploring how these fields can contribute to our understanding of this extraordinary event. It will showcase existing research, highlight promising avenues for future inquiry, and ultimately demonstrate the value of approaching the Maha Kumbh not just as a pilgrimage but as a unique and complex phenomenon that offers a wealth of scientific insights. The aim is to establish a connection between scientific research and spiritual comprehension, cultivating a deeper appreciation for the intricacy and awe of the Maha Kumbh, and its capacity to enhance our comprehension of the human condition.

3. The Premise: Maha Kumbh as a Unique Convergence of Spirituality, Human Experience, and Scientific Inquiry

Unique Convergence of Spirituality

The Maha Kumbh stands as a testament to the enduring power of faith and the human quest for meaning. It is a spectacle of unparalleled scale, a vibrant tapestry woven with threads of ancient mythology, deep-seated traditions, and profound spiritual experiences. However, beyond its readily apparent religious significance, the Maha Kumbh also presents itself as a unique and invaluable site for scientific inquiry. This book is built on the premise that the Maha Kumbh represents a remarkable convergence of spirituality, human experience, and scientific investigation, offering researchers an unprecedented opportunity to explore the complex interplay between these three domains.

This convergence is not merely coincidental; it is inherent in the very nature of the Maha Kumbh. The event brings together millions of individuals, driven by a shared spiritual purpose, creating a microcosm of humanity in its most raw and authentic form. The massive congregation, the intense focus on ritual and devotion, and the unique environment of the temporary tent city create a natural laboratory for scientists to study a wide range of phenomena, from individual behaviour within a crowd to the collective impact of faith on well-being.

The spiritual dimension of the Maha Kumbh is undeniable. It is a pilgrimage of immense significance, rooted in ancient mythology and driven by a deep desire for spiritual purification and liberation. The rituals, the chants, and the collective bathing in the sacred waters—all these elements contribute to a powerful and transformative experience for the pilgrims. This spiritual intensity, however, does not preclude scientific inquiry. Rather, it provides a unique context for exploring the very nature of spiritual experience, the psychological impact of faith, and the potential benefits of religious practices. Scientists can investigate how these spiritual experiences manifest in the human brain; how they influence emotions and behaviour; and how they contribute to a sense of meaning and purpose in life.

Human Experience

The human experience at the Maha Kumbh is multifaceted and profound. Pilgrims embark on this journey for a variety of reasons, each with their own personal motivations and aspirations. They endure hardships, travel long distances, and immerse themselves in a sea of humanity, all in pursuit of spiritual growth. This shared experience creates a powerful sense of community and belonging. Researchers can study the social dynamics of the Mela, observing how individuals interact within the crowd, how social norms are established and maintained, and how collective emotions are expressed. The Maha Kumbh provides a unique opportunity to understand human behaviour in a large, real-world setting, shedding light on phenomena such as crowd psychology, collective identity, and the influence of social context on individual actions.

Scientific Inquiry

The scientific inquiry at the Maha Kumbh is not intended to replace or diminish the spiritual significance of the event. Instead, it aims to complement our understanding of this extraordinary phenomenon by exploring its various dimensions through a scientific lens. By applying the tools and methods of scientific investigation, we can gain new insights into the human condition, the power of collective experience, and the intricate relationship between mind, body, and spirit. The Maha Kumbh, therefore, becomes a meeting point for ancient traditions and modern science, a place where faith and reason can coexist and inform each other.

Convergence

The convergence of spirituality, human experience, and scientific inquiry is what makes the Maha Kumbh such a compelling subject for research. It is a place where the intangible aspects of human existence, such as faith and spirituality, intersect with the tangible realities of human behaviour and social interactions. It is a place where the individual and the collective are inextricably linked, where personal journeys of faith unfold within a vast ocean of humanity. And it is a place where science can shed light on these complex dynamics, offering new perspectives on the human experience and the enduring power of the human spirit.

The book will explore this convergence in detail, examining the various ways in which scientific inquiry can contribute to our understanding of the Maha Kumbh. The specific research questions, methodologies, and insights will be discussed. The premise is that by embracing the Maha Kumbh as a unique convergence of spirituality, human experience, and scientific inquiry, we can unlock new knowledge about ourselves and the world around us while also deepening our appreciation for the rich tapestry of human existence.

4. Target Audience: Academics, Researchers, and General Readers

This book has been crafted with a diverse audience in mind, recognising the multifaceted appeal of the Maha Kumbh and the broad spectrum of individuals who might be interested in exploring its complexities. It aims to bridge the gap between academic rigour and accessibility, making the fascinating intersection of spirituality, human experience, and scientific inquiry at the Kumbh Mela engaging and informative for academics, researchers, and general readers alike.

Academics:

For academics, this book serves as a comprehensive resource and a springboard for further investigation. It offers a structured overview of the existing literature on the Maha Kumbh, synthesising research findings from various disciplines, including sociology, anthropology, psychology, religious studies, environmental science, and public health. It aims to provide a critical analysis of the current state of knowledge, highlighting key themes, debates, and methodological approaches. The book also identifies gaps in the existing research and suggests promising avenues for future inquiry. It is intended to be a valuable reference for scholars studying large-scale gatherings, religious phenomena, crowd dynamics, the impact of faith on health, and the intersection of science and spirituality. The book's extensive bibliography and detailed referencing will facilitate further exploration of specific topics and provide a solid foundation for academic research. Moreover, the book's interdisciplinary approach encourages academics to consider the Maha Kumbh from multiple perspectives, fostering cross-disciplinary collaboration and promoting a more holistic understanding of this complex event.

Researchers:

Researchers, whether affiliated with academic institutions or independent scholars, will find this book a valuable tool for their work. It not only provides a theoretical framework for understanding the Maha Kumbh but also offers practical guidance for conducting research in this unique setting. The book discusses the logistical challenges of studying a large-scale event like the Kumbh Mela, including issues related to data collection, participant recruitment, ethical considerations, and access to resources. It also highlights the potential for innovative research methodologies, such as using mobile technology to track crowd movements, employing social network analysis to study social interactions, and utilising physiological measures to assess the impact of spiritual practices on the human body. By showcasing successful research projects conducted at previous Kumbh Melas, the book inspires researchers to develop new and creative approaches to studying this fascinating phenomenon. It encourages researchers to move beyond traditional disciplinary boundaries and embrace interdisciplinary collaboration to gain a more comprehensive understanding of the Maha Kumbh.

General Readers:

This book caters not only to the academic and research communities, but also to the intellectually curious general reader. It acknowledges that the Maha Kumbh holds a certain fascination for anyone interested in human behaviour, cultural phenomena, and the enduring power of faith. The book avoids overly technical jargon and presents complex scientific concepts in a clear and accessible manner. It aims to make the research findings engaging and relevant to a wider audience, demonstrating the practical implications of scientific inquiry for understanding the world around us. The book tells the story of the Maha Kumbh in a compelling way, weaving together historical context, mythological narratives, personal accounts, and scientific insights. It offers a deeper understanding of the event beyond its surface appearance, revealing the complex interplay of factors that contribute to its significance. For general readers, this book provides a window into the world of the Kumbh Mela, offering a unique perspective that combines spiritual appreciation with scientific curiosity. It encourages readers to think critically about the relationship between faith and reason and to appreciate the value of both spiritual experience and scientific inquiry in understanding the human condition.

In essence, this book strives to be more than just a dry academic treatise. It aims to be a compelling narrative, a source of inspiration, and a valuable resource for anyone interested in exploring the fascinating intersection of spirituality, human experience, and scientific inquiry at the Maha Kumbh. It seeks to inform, educate, and inspire, fostering a deeper appreciation for the complexity and wonder of this extraordinary event.

CHAPTER 2: PRAYAGRAJ: A ONCE-IN-THREE-GENERATIONS OPPORTUNITY

1. The Unique Nature of the Maha Kumbh in Prayagraj

The Kumbh Mela, a colossal pilgrimage held every twelve years, rotates among four sacred locations in India: Haridwar, Prayagraj (formerly Allahabad), Nashik, and Ujjain. While each location holds immense religious significance, the Kumbh Mela held in Prayagraj stands apart, occupying a position of unparalleled reverence and spiritual importance. This chapter delves into the unique nature of the Maha Kumbh in Prayagraj, exploring the confluence of factors that elevate it above other iterations of this grand festival.

The Triveni Sangam: A Confluence of the Sacred:

The most prominent factor distinguishing the Prayagraj Kumbh is its location at the Triveni Sangam, the confluence of three sacred rivers: the Ganges, the Yamuna, and the mythical Saraswati. This meeting point is not merely a geographical intersection; it is a space imbued with profound spiritual meaning. Hindu scriptures and ancient traditions describe the Sangam as a place where the earthly and the divine realms intersect, a gateway to spiritual purification and liberation. The act of bathing at the Sangam during the auspicious period of the Kumbh is believed to cleanse one's sins, break the cycle of reincarnation (moksha), and bring one closer to spiritual enlightenment. This belief is deeply ingrained in Hindu cosmology and is the primary driver for the immense multitudes that congregate at Prayagraj.

The Triveni Sangam is not simply a confluence of physical rivers; it represents a confluence of spiritual currents, a meeting point of ancient wisdom and contemporary faith. The Ganges, revered as a goddess (Ganga Ma), is considered the river of heaven, while the Yamuna, associated with Lord Krishna, symbolises divine love and devotion. The mythical Saraswati, though no longer visible, is believed to represent knowledge, purity, and the flow of consciousness. The union of these three rivers at Prayagraj creates a powerful vortex of spiritual energy, making the Kumbh Mela held here an exceptionally potent occasion for spiritual seekers.

Mythological and Historical Resonance:

The spiritual significance of the Prayagraj Kumbh is further amplified by its deep roots in Hindu mythology and history. The Sangam finds mention in ancient epics like the Ramayana and the Mahabharata, solidifying its place in Hindu cosmology. These texts narrate stories of sages, deities, and heroes visiting the Sangam for purification and spiritual advancement, reinforcing its sanctity and importance. The legend of the Samudra Manthan, the churning of the cosmic ocean, is particularly relevant. It is believed that drops of Amrita, the nectar of immortality, fell at the

Sangam during the tussle between gods and demons, imbuing the waters with divine grace. This mythical connection elevates the Prayagraj Kumbh to a level of spiritual importance that surpasses the Kumbh Melas held at other locations.

Prayagraj, formerly known as Allahabad, also boasts a rich historical heritage. Its strategic location at the confluence of rivers has made it an important centre of trade, culture, and spirituality for centuries. From Mauryas and Guptas to Mughals and British, the city has seen many empires rise and fall, marking the city, contributing to its cosmopolitan character and its rich tapestry of traditions. The Mughal emperor Akbar built a magnificent fort at the Sangam, which stands as a testament to the city's historical significance. This historical depth adds another layer of meaning to the Kumbh Mela, connecting the contemporary celebration to a long lineage of spiritual practice and cultural exchange.

A Microcosm of Hindu Dharma:

The Prayagraj Kumbh is not just a religious event; it is a vibrant expression of Hindu culture and tradition. It brings together millions of pilgrims from all walks of life, transcending caste, social status, and linguistic barriers. The Mela provides a platform for religious discourse, with countless saints, gurus, and spiritual leaders holding discourses, leading prayers, and sharing their wisdom. The Mela serves as a platform for diverse Hindu traditions, showcasing the rich tapestry of beliefs, practices, and philosophies that constitute Hinduism. The Prayagraj Kumbh, therefore, is a microcosm of Hindu Dharma, a living embodiment of its spiritual depth and cultural diversity.

The sheer scale of the gathering is awe-inspiring. Millions of people converge on Prayagraj, creating a temporary tent city of unprecedented size. This ephemeral city, known as Kalpavas, becomes a bustling hub of activity, with pilgrims engaging in rituals, attending religious discourses, and interacting with fellow devotees. The atmosphere is charged with spiritual energy, creating a sense of collective devotion and shared purpose. The Prayagraj Kumbh is a testament to the enduring power of faith and the human quest for meaning.

The King of Kumbh Melas:

People often refer to the Maha Kumbh at Prayagraj as the "king" of all Kumbh Melas.. This title reflects its unparalleled spiritual significance and the immense crowds it attracts. As the holiest and most important Kumbh Mela, pilgrims come from across India and abroad. The sheer number of people who participate in the Prayagraj Kumbh is a testament to its spiritual power and its cultural resonance. It is an event that occurs only once in three generations, making it an exceptional occasion. This exceptional occasion's rarity intensifies its significance for the pilgrims, transforming it into a life-changing journey that fulfils their spiritual aspirations.

The unique nature of the Prayagraj Kumbh stems from the confluence of several factors: the sacred Triveni Sangam, its deep roots in mythology and history, its role as a microcosm of Hindu Dharma, and its status as the "king" of all Kumbh Melas. These factors combine to create an event of unparalleled spiritual significance, attracting millions of pilgrims and offering a unique opportunity for spiritual purification and cultural exchange. The Maha Kumbh at Prayagraj, therefore, is not just another religious festival; it is a phenomenon that embodies the essence of Hindu faith and tradition.

2. Maha Kumbh in Prayagraj: Historical and Geographical Context

The Maha Kumbh Mela held in Prayagraj, situated at the confluence of the Ganges, Yamuna, and the mythical Saraswati rivers (the Triveni Sangam), is not merely a contemporary religious festival. It is an event deeply rooted in the historical and geographical fabric of the region, drawing its significance from centuries of tradition, mythology, and the unique characteristics of its location. Understanding this historical and geographical context is crucial to appreciating the profound spiritual and cultural importance of the Maha Kumbh in Prayagraj.

Ancient Roots and Mythological Connections:

Prayagraj, formerly known as Allahabad, has a rich and ancient history, with its origins obscured by the passage of time. The Triveni Sangam itself is not just a geographical feature; it is a point of powerful symbolic convergence, mentioned in ancient Hindu scriptures like the Ramayana and the Mahabharata. These epics narrate stories of sages, deities, and heroes visiting the Sangam for purification and spiritual advancement, establishing its sanctity and importance from time immemorial. The Sangam is thus woven into the very fabric of Hindu mythology, its waters believed to possess divine grace and the power to cleanse sins.

The legend of the Samudra Manthan, the churning of the cosmic ocean, further enhances the mythological significance of the Sangam. According to this narrative, drops of Amrita, the nectar of immortality, fell at the Sangam during the tussle between gods and demons, imbuing the waters with divine grace. This mythical connection elevates the Prayagraj Kumbh to a level of spiritual importance that surpasses other Kumbh Melas. The belief that bathing at the Sangam during the auspicious time of the Kumbh can bestow spiritual liberation (moksha) stems from these ancient myths and reinforces the profound faith associated with this event.

Historical Connotations

The name Prayagraj itself has historical connotations. Prayaga, which means "confluence," is believed to have inspired the name, emphasising the significance of the river's meeting.

The name was inspired by the significance of the river's meeting. The area around the Sangam continued to be known as Prayag, reflecting the enduring connection to its ancient roots. This continuity of nomenclature signifies the enduring importance of the Sangam as a sacred site, even through periods of changing political and cultural landscapes.

Geographical Significance of the Triveni Sangam:

The geographical context of Prayagraj is as crucial to the Kumbh's significance as its mythological associations. The Triveni Sangam is not just a meeting point of three rivers; it is a confluence of sacred energies. The Ganges and Yamuna, two of the most revered rivers in Hinduism, meet at Prayagraj, creating a visually striking and spiritually potent confluence. The mythical Saraswati, though no longer physically visible, is believed to join the other two rivers at the Sangam, adding another layer of sanctity to the location.

The Ganges, revered as a goddess (Ganga Ma), is considered the river of heaven, its waters believed to possess purifying powers. The Yamuna, associated with Lord Krishna, symbolises divine love and devotion. The mythical Saraswati, though invisible, represents knowledge, purity, and the flow of consciousness. The union of these three rivers at Prayagraj is not just a geographical phenomenon; it is a cosmic event, a meeting of divine forces that amplifies the spiritual significance of the Kumbh held here.

The geographical features of the region also contribute to the importance of Prayagraj. The fertile plains surrounding the Sangam, nourished by the waters of the rivers, have supported human habitation for millennia. The abundance of water has made the region a centre of agriculture, trade, and culture, contributing to its prosperity and importance as a pilgrimage site. The geography of the region, therefore, is not merely a backdrop to the Kumbh; it is an integral part of its significance, shaping its history, its culture, and its spiritual meaning.

Historical Evolution of Prayagraj:

Prayagraj's history is intricately intertwined with elements from diverse eras and empires. From ancient kingdoms to Mughal rule and British colonialism, the city has witnessed the ebb and flow of power, each leaving its imprint on the city's character. The Mughal emperor Akbar built a magnificent fort at the Sangam, which stands as a testament to the city's historical importance. The fort, strategically located at the confluence of the rivers, served as a symbol of Mughal power and a center of administration.

The historical evolution of Prayagraj is intertwined with the development of the Kumbh Mela itself. While the exact origins of the Mela are debated, it is clear that it has been held at the Sangam for centuries, its traditions evolving and adapting over time. The historical context of Prayagraj, therefore, is not just a backdrop to the Kumbh; it is an integral part of its history, shaping its traditions and contributing to its enduring significance.

Connecting Past, Present, and Future:

The Maha Kumbh in Prayagraj is not just a contemporary event; it is a continuation of ancient traditions, a celebration of faith that has been passed down through generations. The historical and geographical context of Prayagraj provides a deeper understanding of the Kumbh's significance, connecting the present-day celebration to its ancient roots and its unique location. The Triveni Sangam, with its mythological associations and its geographical importance, serves as a focal point for the Mela, drawing pilgrims from all walks of life and inspiring a sense of collective devotion.

The Maha Kumbh in Prayagraj, therefore, is a confluence

of past, present, and future. It is a celebration of ancient traditions, a reflection of contemporary faith, and a symbol of enduring spiritual values. The historical and geographical context of Prayagraj provides the foundation for this extraordinary event, shaping its significance and contributing to its enduring appeal. Understanding this context allows us to appreciate the Maha Kumbh not just as a religious festival but as a cultural phenomenon deeply embedded in the history and geography of the region, a testament to the enduring power of faith and the human quest for meaning.

3. Highlighting the rarity and significance of the Maha Kumbh in Prayagraj

The Maha Kumbh Mela, a colossal pilgrimage and festival, is a rare and significant event in itself, occurring only once every twelve years. However, within this cycle, the Kumbh Mela held in Prayagraj stands out as particularly exceptional. Its location at the Triveni Sangam, the confluence of the Ganges, Yamuna, and the mythical Saraswati rivers, elevates its spiritual significance and amplifies its rarity. This chapter delves into the factors that make the Maha Kumbh in Prayagraj a unique and once-in-a-lifetime opportunity for most individuals.

The Twelve-Year Cycle: A Rare Phenomenon:

The Kumbh Mela's twelve-year cycle is determined by the intricate alignment of celestial bodies, specifically the positions of Jupiter, the Sun, and the Moon in relation to specific zodiac signs. This astrological configuration is believed to occur at these specific intervals, marking a particularly auspicious time for ritual bathing and the attainment of spiritual liberation. This precise celestial timing makes the Kumbh Mela a rare phenomenon, occurring only when the planetary positions align to create this potent spiritual window.

This twelve-year cycle contributes to the significance of

the Kumbh Mela in several ways. Firstly, it builds anticipation and reverence for the event. The long wait between Kumbh Melas allows devotees to prepare themselves spiritually and physically for the pilgrimage. Secondly, it reinforces the belief in the power of astrological influences on human affairs. The fact that the Mela occurs at specific intervals dictated by celestial movements strengthens the faith in the interconnectedness of the cosmos and human destiny.

Prayagraj: The King of Kumbh Melas:

While all Kumbh Melas are significant, the one held in Prayagraj holds a special place in the hearts of Hindus. Its location at the Triveni Sangam makes it the most sacred of all the Kumbh Melas. The confluence of the Ganges and Yamuna and the presence of the mythical Saraswati create a powerful vortex of spiritual energy. This unique geographical and mythological context elevates the Prayagraj Kumbh to a level of importance that surpasses other Kumbh Melas.

The Prayagraj Kumbh is often referred to as the "king" of all Kumbh Melas, attracting the largest crowds and holding the highest spiritual importance. As the most auspicious and effective Kumbh Mela, it draws pilgrims from across India and abroad. The Prayagraj Kumbh is a testament to its spiritual power and its cultural resonance.

The Maha Kumbh: A Once-in-Three-Generations Event:

Within the twelve-year cycle of the Kumbh Mela, the Maha Kumbh, held in Prayagraj, stands out as an exceptionally rare event. While the Kumbh Mela occurs every twelve years, the Maha Kumbh, with its heightened spiritual significance at the Triveni Sangam, occurs only once in approximately 144 years. This rarity amplifies its significance for the pilgrims, making it a unique occasion.

The Maha Kumbh's infrequency makes it a once-in-three-generation event for most individuals. The chances of experiencing this particular Kumbh Mela are slim, making it a pilgrimage of a lifetime for those who are fortunate enough to attend. This rarity adds to the sense of urgency and importance associated with the event. Pilgrims believe that participating in the Maha Kumbh at Prayagraj can bestow exceptional spiritual merit and bring them closer to moksha.

Amplified Significance and Spiritual Potency:

The rarity of the Maha Kumbh in Prayagraj contributes to its amplified significance and spiritual potency. The long wait between these events allows for the accumulation of anticipation and reverence. The belief that this particular Kumbh is more efficacious than others further strengthens the faith and devotion of the pilgrims. The convergence of these factors creates an atmosphere of intense spiritual energy, making the Maha Kumbh a truly transformative experience.

The Maha Kumbh's rarity also makes it a significant cultural and social event. It is a time when families come together, when communities reconnect, and when traditions are reaffirmed. The shared experience of participating in this rare event strengthens social bonds and fosters a sense of collective identity. The Maha Kumbh, therefore, is not just a religious festival; it is a cultural phenomenon that reflects the rich diversity and spiritual depth of Hinduism.

A Window into Eternity:

The Maha Kumbh in Prayagraj, with its unique combination of rarity, spiritual significance, and cultural resonance, offers pilgrims a window into eternity. It is an opportunity to connect with ancient traditions, to immerse oneself in a sea of devotion, and to experience the transformative power of faith. The event's rarity enhances its significance, transforming it into a once-in-a-lifetime pilgrimage for those who are fortunate enough to participate.

The Maha Kumbh's infrequency also serves as a reminder of the transient nature of human life. The fact that this event occurs only once in approximately 144 years underscores the importance of making the most of this rare opportunity. It encourages pilgrims to reflect on their own lives, to seek spiritual growth, and to connect with something larger than themselves.

In conclusion, the Maha Kumbh in Prayagraj is a rare and significant event, occurring only once in approximately 144 years. Its location at the Triveni Sangam, its association with ancient mythology, and its amplified spiritual potency make it the most important of all Kumbh Melas. This once-in-three-generations event offers pilgrims a unique opportunity for spiritual purification, cultural exchange, and a profound connection with their faith. The Maha Kumbh's enduring appeal stems from its rarity, transforming it into a once-in-a-lifetime pilgrimage that exemplifies the enduring power of faith.

4. Why this particular Maha Kumbh in Prayagraj offers exceptional research potential

The Maha Kumbh Mela held in Prayagraj, with its unique confluence of spiritual significance, massive scale, and rich cultural context, presents an unparalleled opportunity for scientific research across a multitude of disciplines. The very factors that make this event religiously significant also create a natural laboratory for researchers, offering insights into human behaviour, social dynamics, public health, environmental science, and even the nature of belief itself. This chapter will delve into the specific reasons why this particular Maha Kumbh offers exceptional research potential.

Scale and Diversity: A Natural Laboratory for Social Sciences:

The sheer scale of the Maha Kumbh in Prayagraj is staggering, with millions of pilgrims congregating at the Triveni Sangam. This massive gathering gives researchers a unique opportunity to study human behaviour on an unprecedented scale. The diversity of the pilgrim population, encompassing individuals from all walks of life, across different social strata, linguistic groups, and cultural backgrounds, further enriches the research potential. This diversity allows researchers to investigate a wide range of social phenomena, from crowd dynamics and collective behaviour to the formation and maintenance of social norms in a temporary megacity.

Researchers can study how individuals navigate within such a large crowd, how social interactions unfold, and how collective emotions are expressed and amplified. Maha Kumbh offers a natural setting to observe and analyse crowd psychology, leadership dynamics, and the spread of information and ideas among a large population. The temporary nature of the Kumbh Mela also allows researchers to study the formation and dissolution of temporary communities, the emergence of social structures, and the impact of shared experiences on individual and collective identity.

Spiritual Context: Exploring the Impact of Faith:

The intense spiritual atmosphere of the Maha Kumbh provides a unique opportunity to explore the impacts of faith and religious practices on human behaviour and well-being. Researchers can investigate the psychological and physiological effects of ritualistic bathing, chanting, meditation, and other religious practices. How do these practices influence stress levels, immune function, and mental health? How does participation in a mass religious event affect an individual's sense of belonging, purpose, and meaning? We can explore these questions in this context.

The Maha Kumbh also offers a platform to study the social and cultural dimensions of faith. Researchers can investigate how religious beliefs and practices are transmitted and reinforced within a community; how religious identity is constructed and negotiated; and how religious experiences shape individual and collective behaviour. The intense focus on spiritual practices during the Kumbh Mela provides a unique window into the role of religion in human life and its impact on individual and social well-being.

Public Health Challenges: Opportunities for Epidemiological Research:

The congregation of millions of people from diverse backgrounds, often with varying levels of access to healthcare and sanitation, presents unique public health challenges. The Maha Kumbh, therefore, becomes a site of potential epidemiological research. Researchers can study the spread of infectious diseases during the Mela, gaining valuable insights into disease transmission dynamics in large gatherings. This research can inform public health strategies for managing large-scale events and preventing disease outbreaks.

The Maha Kumbh also offers an opportunity to study the health behaviours of pilgrims, their access to healthcare services, and the impact of the pilgrimage on their physical and mental health. Researchers can investigate the prevalence of various health conditions, the utilisation of health services, and the effectiveness of public health interventions during the Mela. This research can contribute to improving public health practices and ensuring the well-being of pilgrims during large gatherings.

Environmental Impact: Studying Sustainability at Scale:

The sheer volume of waste generated by millions of pilgrims, the management of sanitation, and the potential impact on the water quality of the sacred rivers are all critical environmental concerns. The Maha Kumbh provides a unique opportunity to study the environmental impact of large-scale gatherings and to develop sustainable solutions for managing waste, conserving water resources, and protecting the environment.

Researchers can investigate the effectiveness of different waste management strategies, the impact of human activity on the water quality of the Sangam, and the ecological footprint of the Mela. This research can lead to innovative solutions for minimising the environmental impact of large events and promoting sustainable practices in other contexts, as well.

Interdisciplinary Collaboration: A Holistic Approach:

The Maha Kumbh, with its complex interplay of social, cultural, spiritual, and environmental factors, necessitates an interdisciplinary approach to research. Researchers from various disciplines, including sociology, anthropology, psychology, medicine, environmental science, and religious studies, can collaborate to gain a more holistic understanding of this multifaceted event. Interdisciplinary research can lead to more comprehensive insights and more effective solutions to the challenges posed by large-scale gatherings.

The Maha Kumbh in Prayagraj, therefore, offers exceptional research potential due to its massive scale, its diverse population, its intense spiritual context, and its complex environmental challenges. It is a natural laboratory for researchers to study a wide range of phenomena related to human behaviour, social dynamics, public health, environmental sustainability, and the impact of faith on well-being. By embracing the Maha Kumbh as a site of scientific inquiry, we can gain valuable insights into the human condition and develop more effective strategies for addressing the challenges of our time.

CHAPTER 3: A MICROCOSM OF SEEKERS: THE DIVERSE ASSEMBLAGE

1. Introduction to the various groups, including pandits, sadhus, saints, sages, agoris, sanyasis, and naga sadhus.

The Maha Kumbh in Prayagraj is a meticulously structured gathering of diverse spiritual practitioners, each adding their unique contribution to the rich tapestry of the event. This chapter introduces us to the primary groups that form the core of this spiritual microcosm: pandits, sadhus, saints, sages, agoris, sanyasis, and naga sadhus. Understanding each group's role, function, and place within the broader context of the Maha Kumbh is crucial for appreciating the sheer depth and complexity of the event. Let us delve into the diverse spiritual figures who populate the Maha Kumbh, each contributing to the rich tapestry of traditions and beliefs that make this event so unique.

Pandits:

Pandits are Hindu scholars and priests, well-versed in ancient scriptures like the Vedas, Upanishads, and Puranas. They are the custodians of religious knowledge, acting as interpreters of sacred texts and performers of rituals. At the

Maha Kumbh, Pandits play a crucial role in guiding pilgrims through the complex rituals, explaining the significance of various ceremonies, and offering spiritual counsel. They often set up temporary stalls or pandals where they engage with pilgrims, answering questions, reciting mantras, and performing pujas (worship ceremonies). Pandits are not necessarily renunciates; many have families and lead regular lives while dedicating a portion of their time to religious duties. Their presence at the Kumbh is essential for maintaining the traditional practices and ensuring the smooth conduct of religious observances. They are the link to the ancient wisdom of Hinduism, preserving and transmitting it to the present generation.

Sadhus:

Sadhus are Hindu ascetics who have renounced worldly life to pursue spiritual liberation. They often live a simple life, detached from material possessions and dedicated to meditation, prayer, and the study of scriptures. Sadhus can be categorised into various sects and orders, each with its own unique philosophy and practice. At the Maha Kumbh, Sadhus gather in large numbers, often residing in temporary camps or kutias. They engage in religious discourses, lead prayers, and share their spiritual insights with pilgrims. Many Sadhus are known for their extreme austerities and practices, showcasing their dedication to spiritual discipline. Their presence at the Kumbh adds to the spiritual atmosphere, inspiring pilgrims with their devotion and renunciation. The Sadhus represent the path of renunciation and self-realization, embodying the pursuit of spiritual freedom.

Saints:

In the context of the Maha Kumbh, the term "saint" generally refers to individuals who have attained a high level of spiritual realisation. They are often revered for their wisdom, compassion, and miraculous powers. Saints may or may not be renunciates; some lead regular lives while others live as ascetics. They are often considered living embodiments of divine qualities, serving as role models for spiritual seekers. At the Kumbh, saints attract large followings, delivering discourses, answering questions, and offering guidance to pilgrims. Their presence is a source of inspiration and blessings for the devotees. Saints are often seen as bridges between the divine and the human, offering a path to spiritual growth and enlightenment.

Sages:

Sages, like saints, are revered for their wisdom and spiritual insight. The term "sage" often implies a deep understanding of philosophical and metaphysical truths. Sages are often associated with ancient times, with many Hindu scriptures attributed to various sages. At the Kumbh, contemporary sages share their wisdom through discourses, writings, and interactions with pilgrims. They may or may not be renunciates, but their lives are typically dedicated to the pursuit of knowledge and spiritual understanding. Sages represent the intellectual and philosophical tradition within Hinduism, offering insights into the nature of reality and the path to self-discovery.

Agoris:

The Aghoris are a distinct and somewhat controversial sect within Hinduism. They are known for their extreme practices, which often involve living in cremation grounds, consuming human flesh (in ritual contexts), and meditating on death and impermanence. Aghoris believe that by confronting death and decay, they can transcend the fear of death and attain spiritual liberation. Their practices are often misunderstood and viewed with apprehension by the general public. At the Kumbh, Aghoris may be present, but they typically keep to themselves, engaging in their unique practices. Their presence serves as a reminder of the diverse and sometimes extreme expressions of spiritual seeking within Hinduism.

Sanyasis:

Sanyasis are individuals who have formally renounced worldly life, taking vows of detachment and dedicating themselves to spiritual pursuits. They often wear ochre-colored robes, symbolised by their renunciation. Sanyasis can belong to various orders and sects, each with its own specific practices and philosophies. At the Maha Kumbh, Sanyasis gather in large numbers, engaging in religious discourses, leading prayers, and sharing their spiritual experiences. They often reside in ashrams or camps, maintaining a disciplined lifestyle of meditation, study, and service. Sanyasis represent the path of complete renunciation, dedicating their lives entirely to the pursuit of spiritual liberation.

Naga Sadhus:

Naga Sadhus are a unique and highly visible group of ascetics who are known for their extreme renunciation and their association with the Naga sect. They often live naked or semi-naked, their bodies covered in ash. Naga Sadhus are known for their martial skills and their fierce devotion to Lord Shiva. They are often seen as protectors of the Hindu faith. At the Kumbh, Naga Sadhus play a prominent role, participating in ceremonial processions and displaying their spiritual prowess. Their presence is a spectacle that draws considerable attention, adding to the mystique and grandeur of the Maha Kumbh. Naga Sadhus represent a tradition of warrior-ascetics, combining spiritual discipline with martial arts and devotion. This introduction sets the stage for understanding the diverse spiritual landscape of the Maha Kumbh. Each of these groups contributes to the rich tapestry of the event.

2. The diversity of the groups' backgrounds and practices:

The diversity of the groups at the Maha Kumbh is not just a matter of differing titles; it reflects a multitude of backgrounds, philosophies, and practices that are as varied as the spiritual paths themselves. Each group carries its unique traditions, beliefs, and approaches to spiritual liberation, creating a complex and fascinating microcosm of spiritual life.

Pandits, for example, typically come from Brahmin families, often with generations of scholastic lineage. Their practices are primarily focused on scriptural study, ritual performance, and the transmission of knowledge, making them the guardians of religious orthodoxy. Deeply embedded in societal structures, they uphold the traditional Hindu worldview and often serve as advisors and educators for laypeople.

Sadhus come from diverse social backgrounds, and their practices vary significantly based on their sectarian affiliation. Some follow strict ascetic disciplines, renouncing worldly pleasures and practicing yoga, meditation, or austerity.

Others engage in devotional practices, worshipping deities through prayers, songs, and rituals. The varied paths within the Sadhu tradition demonstrate the diverse ways in which individuals seek moksha, or liberation, from the cycle of birth and death.

Saints, on the other hand, often come from varied backgrounds and life experiences that led them to spirituality. Their practices revolve around deep meditation, compassion, and selfless service. Saints may be revered for their unique spiritual insights and their unwavering devotion to the divine.

Sages, sometimes viewed synonymously with saints, also present a broad spectrum of backgrounds. Their path to wisdom is often characterised by years of deep study, contemplation, and, often, solitude, but they are rooted in ancient lineages of spiritual knowledge.

The practices of Agoris are intentionally transgressive, defying societal norms and conventional spiritual practices. They may engage in rituals involving cremation grounds, skulls, and other practices that challenge the concepts of purity and impurity, aiming to transcend the duality of good and evil.

Sanyasis come from all walks of life, and their practices are as diverse as their lineages. Often residing in ashrams or monasteries, they engage in study, meditation, and selfless service, as well as various spiritual disciplines.

The Naga Sadhus are marked by their extreme forms of renunciation. Often naked, they practice strict austerity, with some even engaging in self-mortification as part of their spiritual quest. Their life of detachment from worldly concerns is seen as a path to transcendence, demonstrating a commitment to the divine by relinquishing all forms of material comfort and vanity.

This diversity in background and practice enriches the Maha Kumbh, showcasing the multitude of paths that individuals take towards enlightenment.

3. The confluence of wisdom traditions and spiritual paths at the Maha Kumbh

The Maha Kumbh Mela is more than just a massive gathering of people; it represents a vibrant confluence of diverse wisdom traditions and spiritual paths, a fusion of philosophical schools, ancient lineages, and diverse approaches to spiritual inquiry. This coming together makes a lively intellectual and spiritual ecosystem that provides an unmatched chance for ideas to spread, for learning, and for getting a better sense of the many aspects of spiritual exploration. It is a living library of wisdom, where ancient traditions meet contemporary seekers, fostering a powerful exchange of knowledge and inspiration.

A Symphony of Philosophical Schools:

The Maha Kumbh provides a stage for the grand philosophical schools of Hinduism to engage in a vibrant dialogue. The Maha Kumbh Mela, beyond its vibrant displays of devotion and ritual, serves as a grand stage for a vibrant dialogue between the major philosophical schools of Hinduism. It is a unique opportunity to witness these intricate systems of thought come alive, debated, and discussed in the context of a living spiritual tradition. The presence of learned scholars and renunciates who represent these diverse viewpoints transforms the Kumbh into a crucible of intellectual and spiritual exploration.

Advaita Vedanta: The Non-Dualistic Perspective:

Advaita Vedanta, perhaps the most influential school of Vedanta philosophy, emphasises the non-dual nature of reality. Its core tenet is the oneness of the individual soul (Atman) with the ultimate reality (Brahman). This oneness implies that the apparent distinctions between the self and the universe are ultimately illusory. At the Maha Kumbh, Advaita Vedanta finds expression through learnt scholars who delve into the profound implications of this non-dualistic worldview. They expound upon the intricate philosophical concepts of Maya (illusion), Brahman (absolute reality), and Atman (the individual soul), using logic, scriptural authority, and personal experience to illuminate the path to self-realization. Renunciants, who have dedicated their lives to realising this oneness, often share their insights and experiences, offering practical guidance to those seeking to understand the nature of reality. The Kumbh provides a platform for these Advaita teachers to engage with seekers, answering questions, clarifying doubts, and guiding them toward a deeper understanding of the non-dualistic perspective.

Vishishtadvaita Vedanta: Qualified Non-Dualism:

Vishishtadvaita Vedanta, championed by the philosopher Ramanuja, offers a different perspective on the relationship between the individual soul and God. It proposes a qualified non-dualism, where the individual soul and the world are both part of Brahman but distinct from it. Brahman, in this view, is not an impersonal absolute but a personal God (Ishvara) who is the inner controller and sustainer of all beings. The individual soul, while being a part of Brahman, retains its distinct identity and has the potential to achieve liberation through devotion to God. At the Maha Kumbh, proponents of Vishishtadvaita Vedanta engage in discussions and debates, highlighting the importance of devotion (bhakti) as the primary path to liberation. They emphasise the loving relationship between the individual soul and God, offering a more theistic perspective compared to the strict nondualism of Advaita Vedanta. The Kumbh allows for a deeper understanding of this qualified, non-dualistic perspective, showcasing the nuances of devotional practices and the importance of divine grace on the path to spiritual realisation.

Dvaita Vedanta: The Dualistic Viewpoint:

Dvaita Vedanta, as advocated by Madhvacharya, presents a starkly different worldview, emphasising the eternal distinction between the individual soul and God. It advocates a dualistic perspective, where God (Vishnu) is the supreme being, and individual souls are eternally separate and dependent on Him. In this view, liberation is not the realisation of oneness with Brahman but the attainment of eternal bliss in the service of God. At the Maha Kumbh, followers of Dvaita Vedanta engage in philosophical discussions, highlighting the importance of devotion, righteous conduct, and the grace of God in achieving liberation. They emphasise the personal nature of God and the importance of having a loving relationship with him. The Kumbh gives this dualistic view a place to be shown and talked about, which adds to the field of philosophy and gives people a new way to think about reality and the way to spiritual fulfilment.

A Crucible of Philosophical Exploration:

The presence of these diverse philosophical schools at the Maha Kumbh transforms the event into a crucible of philosophical exploration. The convergence of these different viewpoints allows for a deep and nuanced understanding of Hindu thought. Pilgrims and seekers have the opportunity to engage with these complex ideas, listen to learnt scholars, and reflect on their own philosophical leanings. The Kumbh becomes a space for robust intellectual discourse, where these schools of thought interact, debate, and challenge each other, enriching the philosophical landscape and contributing to the ongoing evolution of Hindu thought. It is a living testament to the intellectual depth and philosophical richness of Hinduism, offering a unique opportunity to explore the diverse paths to understanding the nature of reality, the self, and the divine.

These different philosophical schools make it possible to really look into the subtleties of Hindu thought. They give pilgrims and seekers a chance to interact with these difficult ideas and figure out what their own philosophical leanings are. The Kumbh becomes a space for robust intellectual discourse, where these schools of thought interact, debate, and enrich the philosophical landscape.

A Kaleidoscope of Sects and Deities:

The Mahakumbh Mela is not just a gathering of individuals; it's a confluence of diverse sects within Hinduism, each contributing its own unique flavour to the vibrant spiritual landscape. These sects, with their distinct modes of worship, rituals, and beliefs, create a kaleidoscopic atmosphere, showcasing the multifaceted nature of Hinduism and its inclusive approach to spiritual seeking. The Kumbh becomes a melting pot of devotional expressions, where different paths converge, each leading towards the same ultimate goal.

Shaivism: The Devotees of Lord Shiva:

Shaivism, the worship of Lord Shiva, is one of the oldest and most influential sects within Hinduism. The Shaivites emphasise asceticism, devotion, and the worship of Shiva as a divine masculine principle, representing destruction and transformation. At the Maha Kumbh, Shaivites bring their distinct energy to the Mela. Ascetics, often covered in ash and adorned with matted hair, engage in rigorous spiritual practices, demonstrating their detachment from worldly possessions and their dedication to Shiva. Devotees chant mantras, perform pujas (worship ceremonies), and immerse themselves in the worship of Shiva in his various forms, from the gentle and compassionate to the fierce and powerful. The presence of Shaivites at the Kumbh adds a dimension of intensity and spiritual discipline to the overall atmosphere.

Vaishnavism: The Followers of Lord Vishnu:

Vaishnavism, the worship of Lord Vishnu and his various incarnations, particularly Rama and Krishna, is another major sect within Hinduism. Vaishnavites focus on love, devotion, and the worship of Vishnu as the divine preserver, representing sustenance and protection. At the Maha Kumbh, Vaishnavites add a distinct flavour of bhakti (devotion) to the spiritual landscape. Devotees sing devotional songs (bhajans), dance in ecstasy, and immerse themselves in the stories and teachings of Rama and Krishna. They perform elaborate *pujas* and offer their love and devotion to Vishnu and his incarnations. The presence of

Vaishnavites at the Kumbh creates an atmosphere of love, joy, and devotional fervour.

Shaktism: The Worship of the Divine Feminine

Shaktism, the worship of the divine feminine principle (Shakti) in all its forms, from Durga to Kali, adds another crucial dimension to the rich tapestry of beliefs and practices at the Maha Kumbh. Shaktas believe in the power of the divine mother as the ultimate source of creation, energy, and liberation. They worship Shakti as a female creative force, recognising her ability to both create and destroy. At the Kumbh, Shaktas celebrate the divine feminine through various rituals, including the chanting of mantras, the performance of *pujas*, and the offering of sacrifices (in some traditions). The presence of Shaktism at the Kumbh emphasises the importance of the divine feminine in Hindu cosmology and adds a powerful dimension of feminine energy to the overall spiritual atmosphere.

A Tapestry of Beliefs and Practices:

The presence of these diverse sects, along with numerous other sub-sects and traditions within Hinduism, contributes to the rich tapestry of beliefs and practices at the Maha Kumbh. Each sect brings its unique perspective, its specific rituals, and its distinct understanding of the divine. This diversity is not seen as a source of conflict or division; rather, it is celebrated as a reflection of the multifaceted nature of spiritual seeking. Maha Kumbh becomes a space where these different devotional paths converge, each adding its own flavour to the overall spiritual atmosphere.

The Inclusive Nature of Hinduism:

The presence of these diverse sects at the Kumbh highlights the inclusive and multifaceted character of Hinduism. Hinduism does not prescribe a single path to salvation; it recognises that individuals may have different temperaments, inclinations, and preferences. The multiplicity of sects and traditions within Hinduism reflects this understanding, offering a variety of paths to suit different seekers. The Maha Kumbh becomes a living example of this inclusivity, demonstrating that despite the diversity of beliefs and practices, all paths can ultimately lead to the same goal: spiritual liberation.

A Convergence of Devotional Paths:

The Kumbh serves as a space where these different devotional paths converge. It is a place where Shaivites, Vaishnavites, Shaktas, and followers of other traditions come together, united by their shared faith and their desire for spiritual growth. Different forms of worship, rituals, and beliefs coexist harmoniously at the Kumbh. This convergence of devotional paths creates a powerful spiritual atmosphere, enriching the experience for all who participate. The Maha Kumbh, therefore, is not just a religious festival; it is a celebration of the diversity of spiritual seeking and the inclusive nature of Hinduism.

The Integration of Body, Mind, and Spirit:

The Maha Kumbh Mela is not solely a spectacle of religious fervour; it is also a prominent showcase of ancient Indian traditions that promote holistic well-being: yoga, meditation, and Ayurveda. These practices, deeply intertwined with Indian spirituality, are prominently featured at the Kumbh, offering pilgrims a pathway to harmonise body, mind, and spirit. Their convergence at this massive gathering underscores the integrated approach to self-realisation that is a hallmark of Indian spiritual traditions.

Yoga: Harmonising Body and Mind:

Yoga, with its emphasis on physical postures (asanas), breathing techniques (pranayama), and ethical principles (yamas and niyamas), offers a practical and accessible way to harmonise the body and mind. At the Maha Kumbh, yoga is not just a orm of exercise; it is a spiritual discipline. Numerous camps and workshops are set up, offering instruction in various styles of yoga, from Hatha and Raja Yoga to Kundalini and Ashtanga. Pilgrims can participate in group yoga sessions, learn specific asanas to improve their physical health, and practice pranayama techniques to regulate their breath and calm their minds. The ethical principles of yoga, such as non-violence (ahimsa), truthfulness (satya), and non-stealing (asteya), are also emphasised, promoting a holistic approach to living that extends beyond physical practice. The Kumbh provides a fertile ground for experiencing the transformative power of yoga, not just as a physical discipline but as a pathway to spiritual growth.

Meditation: Cultivating Awareness and Inner Peace:

Meditation, with its focus on cultivating awareness and inner peace, plays a crucial role in the spiritual practices at the Maha Kumbh. Meditation is seen as a means to quiet the incessant chatter of the mind, to connect with deeper levels of consciousness, and to experience the stillness and peace that lies within. At Kumbh, various meditation techniques are taught and practised, ranging from mindfulness meditation to mantra meditation and guided visualisations. Pilgrims can attend meditation sessions led by experienced teachers, learn how to cultivate focus and concentration, and experience the profound benefits of inner stillness. The serene atmosphere of the Kumbh, away from the distractions of daily life, provides an ideal environment for deepening one's meditation practice and experiencing the transformative power of inner peace.

Ayurveda: A Holistic Approach to Well-being:

Ayurveda, the traditional system of medicine originating in India, focuses on balancing doshas (biological energies) and promoting natural healing. It offers a holistic approach to physical and mental well-being—recognising the interconnectedness of body, mind, and spirit. At the Maha Kumbh, Ayurvedic practitioners offer consultations, provide herbal remedies, and educate pilgrims about the principles of Ayurvedic living. Ayurvedic stalls are set up, offering a variety of herbal products, dietary advice, and lifestyle recommendations. Kumbh becomes a platform for promoting Ayurvedic principles by emphasising the importance of a balanced diet, regular exercise, and stress management in maintaining health and well-being.

An integrated approach to self-realisation:

The convergence of yoga, meditation, and Ayurveda at the Maha Kumbh highlights the integrated approach to self-realisation that is characteristic of Indian spirituality. These practices are not seen as separate or isolated; they complement and support each other, working together to promote holistic well-being. Yoga provides a foundation for physical and mental health, preparing the body and mind for deeper spiritual practices. Meditation cultivates awareness, concentration, and inner peace, allowing for a deeper connection with one's inner self. Ayurveda supports physical and mental balance, creating a conducive environment for spiritual growth. The Kumbh becomes a space where pilgrims can experience the synergy of these practices, understanding their interconnectedness and experiencing their combined benefits.

A Space for Learning and Experiencing:

The Maha Kumbh provides a unique opportunity for pilgrims to learn about these ancient Indian traditions, to receive guidance from experts, and to experience their benefits firsthand. The presence of experienced yoga teachers, meditation instructors, and Ayurvedic practitioners creates a rich learning environment. Pilgrims can attend workshops, participate in group sessions, and receive individual consultations. The Kumbh becomes a space for both theoretical understanding and practical experience, allowing pilgrims to deepen their knowledge and integrate these practices into their daily lives. The spiritual atmosphere of the Kumbh, combined with the presence of these ancient traditions, creates a powerful and transformative experience for all who participate.

Lineages of Spiritual Masters: A Flow of Spiritual Energy:

The Maha Kumbh also serves as a gathering place for various lineages of spiritual masters (gurus) and their disciples. These lineages, passed down through generations, carry unique wisdom, practices, and spiritual insights. The Kumbh provides an opportunity for these lineages to come together, share their teachings, and strengthen their bonds. Disciples have the chance to connect with their gurus, receive blessings, and deepen their understanding of their respective traditions. The presence of these diverse lineages creates a powerful flow of spiritual energy at the Kumbh, enriching the atmosphere and inspiring seekers on their spiritual journeys. The Kumbh becomes a space where the wisdom of the ages is transmitted from master to disciple, ensuring the continuity of these ancient traditions.

A Dynamic Exchange of Knowledge and Inspiration:

The confluence of wisdom traditions and spiritual paths at the Maha Kumbh is more than just a physical gathering; it is a meeting of minds and spirits, a dynamic exchange of knowledge and inspiration. It is a space where different traditions interact, learn from one another, and strengthen their own beliefs. Pilgrims have the opportunity to engage with diverse perspectives, to ask questions, and to deepen their understanding of the spiritual path. The Maha Kumbh, therefore, serves as a living library of wisdom, where ancient traditions meet the seekers of today, creating a powerful flow of spiritual energy that nourishes and inspires all who participate. It's a testament to the rich tapestry of spiritual seeking and the enduring human quest for meaning and connection.

4. Maha Kumbh: A Confluence of Enlightened Souls and Profound Perspectives

The Maha Kumbh is not just a pilgrimage for the masses; it is a magnet for enlightened individuals from all corners of India and beyond. It draws sages, saints, and masters who have dedicated their lives to spiritual practices and attained profound levels of self-realisation. These individuals, with their varied backgrounds and unique spiritual perspectives, contribute immensely to the event's transformative potential. Their presence elevates the Maha Kumbh from a mere religious gathering to a powerful platform for spiritual awakening.

The enlightened individuals at the Maha Kumbh come from all backgrounds, from remote Himalayan caves to bustling urban centres. They bring with them not only their personal experiences but also the wisdom of ancient lineages, offering insights that are profound and transformative. Their perspectives provide diverse paths for understanding the ultimate nature of reality. These individuals are not merely passive participants in the Kumbh; they actively engage in sharing their wisdom with the pilgrims and seekers, offering teachings, guidance, and blessings. These interactions provide unparalleled learning opportunities, allowing seekers to gain insights into various paths to enlightenment. The enlightened individuals are often a beacon of hope and inspiration for many presents, showing what is possible through dedicated spiritual practice. Their peaceful demeanour, compassion, and profound wisdom set an example for others to follow on their spiritual journeys.

The Maha Kumbh allows for a collective understanding, with these individuals being essential to the spiritual and intellectual environment of the event. The gathering of enlightened individuals also facilitates interfaith and inter-spiritual dialogues. Individuals from different traditions come together to share their unique insights, contributing to a deeper appreciation for the various approaches to spiritual truth.

The Maha Kumbh serves as a space where diverse spiritual viewpoints are not only tolerated but also celebrated, reflecting the common thread of human seeking across all traditions. This gathering of enlightened individuals elevates the Maha Kumbh from a simple religious gathering to a powerful spiritual phenomenon, making it an unparalleled opportunity for seekers to learn, grow, and discover profound insights. It transforms the Kumbh into a space for learning, transformation, and collective spiritual growth.

CHAPTER 4: ETERNAL SEEKING: THE CORE OF THE KUMBH

1. The nature of seeking and thinking within the various traditions present at the Maha Kumbh:

The Maha Kumbh is not merely a destination; it is a vibrant manifestation of the eternal human quest for meaning, truth, and connection with the divine. The event's essence is rooted in seeking, a drive that permeates the various traditions, sects, and individuals that converge at Prayagraj.

This chapter explores the diverse expressions of seeking and thinking that are present within the rich tapestry of the Kumbh, highlighting the unique approaches and methodologies adopted by various groups.

For the Pandits, the learned scholars of Hindu tradition, the nature of seeking is characterised by a deep engagement with the sacred scriptures—the Vedas, Upanishads, and Puranas. Their pursuit of knowledge involves the rigorous study, memorisation, and interpretation of ancient texts, seeking to understand the profound philosophical truths contained within them. Their intellectual approach to seeking is a structured and methodical exploration of the foundations of Hinduism, and their interpretations shape the understanding and practices of many others at the Kumbh.

The Sadhus, with their diverse backgrounds and spiritual paths, embody the practice of renunciation and detachment as a means of spiritual realisation. Their approach is often rooted in experiential understanding, often employing rigorous asceticism, yoga, meditation, and devotion as methods of self-exploration. Their search for truth often involves a journey into the depths of their own consciousness, exploring the subtle realms of awareness. Sadhus understand the nature of seeking through their own lived experiences, often having renounced material comforts and worldly aspirations.

The Saints and Sages at the Kumbh, with their diverse backgrounds and life experiences, seek wisdom and enlightenment through contemplation, deep meditation, compassion, and selfless service. Their personal transformation is seen as a means to inspire others, and they often embody the values of peace, humility, and love.

The Agoras, whose practices challenge conventional norms, approach seeking through unconventional and often transgressive means. They seek to transcend duality and overcome societal prejudices, believing that true understanding comes from confronting the most challenging and uncomfortable aspects of human existence.

The Sanyasis, having taken vows of renunciation, see seeking as a journey towards liberation from worldly attachments through practices of study, contemplation, and selfless service. Their focus is often on breaking free from the illusion of Maya and realising their true identity as members of the divine.

Lastly, the Naga Sadhus, with their austere practices and detachment from the material world, seek ultimate freedom from the limitations of the physical body. Their journey is often marked by rigorous austerities, designed to conquer the demands of their physical being.

These examples of seeking highlight the diversity of spiritual approaches present at the Kumbh, and while the methods may differ, the underlying aspiration is the same: to discover truth, meaning, and connection with the divine.

This shared purpose makes the Maha Kumbh a focal point for diverse methods of seeking, each contributing to the unique nature of this spiritual event.

2. The perpetual quest for knowledge and enlightenment:

At the heart of the Maha Kumbh lies the perpetual quest for knowledge and enlightenment, an enduring journey that transcends the confines of time, space, and individual identity. This quest is not just a desire for information but also a fundamental longing for wisdom, understanding, and a profound connection with the deeper reality of existence. This pursuit is what makes the Kumbh more than a temporary gathering; it is a powerful expression of the eternal human quest for meaning. For those immersed in the traditions of the Maha Kumbh, knowledge is not an end in itself but rather a tool for self-transformation and spiritual realisation.

The acquisition of knowledge is understood as an essential step on the path to enlightenment, and each individual approaches it in their own unique way. Some seek knowledge through rigorous study of ancient texts, engaging in intense intellectual debates and philosophical discussions. This involves delving into the complex and profound philosophical systems of Hinduism, trying to uncover the layers of meaning contained in the scriptures.

Others seek knowledge through direct experience, undergoing rigorous ascetic practices that push the limits of their physical and mental capabilities. They learn from their bodily experiences, seeking to connect directly with the divine. They seek not just intellectual understanding but visceral, direct knowledge of the ultimate reality.

There are others who focus their attention on cultivating wisdom by learning from masters, teachers, and enlightened individuals who have travelled the path before them and learnt from their experiences. This approach recognises the importance of wisdom passed down through generations—learning from the lived wisdom of others.

In addition to knowledge, the quest for enlightenment at the Maha Kumbh is a journey of spiritual transformation, where they seek to understand the true nature of themselves, the world, and their relationship to the divine. The various practices engaged in, ranging from meditation to devotion, are viewed as different pathways that ultimately lead to the same destination—a realisation of the ultimate truth.

The Kumbh is therefore understood as an aid to self-discovery, which allows seekers to come into contact with those who have found deep understanding and encourages them in their journeys. The atmosphere of the Maha Kumbh itself is thought to enhance this pursuit, creating an environment where one can be freed from the distractions and concerns of the mundane, immersing themselves completely in the search for truth.

The spiritual nature of the environment, combined with the presence of like-minded individuals, helps to create a supportive space for the pursuit of knowledge and enlightenment. The perpetual nature of this quest ensures that the Kumbh remains a dynamic and evolving experience, where each pilgrim contributes to the collective pursuit of understanding.

In essence, the Maha Kumbh is a celebration of the human spirit's unyielding desire to know, to understand, and to connect with the deeper truths of existence.

3. How this environment fosters a deeper understanding of human consciousness and the pursuit of truth:

The Maha Kumbh at Prayagraj provides a unique environment that serves as an amplifier for the quest for self-understanding and the pursuit of truth. The convergence of millions seeking spiritual growth creates an atmosphere charged with an intense focus on consciousness, making it a powerful catalyst for inner exploration.

The unique elements that comprise the Maha Kumbh, from the energy of the Sangam to the presence of so many enlightened individuals, all amplify the seeker's potential for growth.

Firstly, the intense concentration of spiritual practice creates an environment that facilitates a deeper understanding of human consciousness. The collective energy of millions of individuals engaged in meditation, rituals, and other spiritual practices generates a powerful field of awareness, making it easier for individuals to turn their attention inwards. This amplified focus on consciousness opens the door to profound inner experiences and realisations. This environment helps an individual identify the underlying unity that connects all beings, creating a sense of interconnectedness and shared human experience.

The presence of enlightened individuals has a powerful influence on those who have come to the Kumbh, providing an opportunity to witness the transformative power of spiritual realisation. Their wisdom, teachings, and very presence serve as an inspiration and encouragement, allowing the seeker to witness the possibilities of enlightenment. Through interactions with those who have experienced profound spiritual awakenings, seekers can gain unique insights into the nature of consciousness and the pathway to enlightenment.

The Maha Kumbh's very structure challenges conventional ways of thinking, eliminating many distractions from daily life. It is a space where many spiritual seekers are encouraged to explore unconventional paths and challenge preconceived notions about the self, society, and the nature of reality. This is not merely a gathering of like-minded individuals; it is also a space where individuals are challenged to expand their own understanding and beliefs.

The act of pilgrimage itself is a powerful tool for self-reflection and inner exploration, where individuals move away from their everyday life to an environment specifically crafted to facilitate a spiritual journey. This journey is not just physical; it also encourages an internal journey, allowing for the opportunity to gain clarity of mind. Overall, this environment at the Maha Kumbh fosters introspection and reflection and encourages individuals to ask difficult questions about the human experience, facilitating a deeper understanding of themselves and the world around them.

This environment acts as a catalyst for the pursuit of truth, both personal and universal, and allows the seeker to question their assumptions, expand their horizons, and embrace a deeper understanding of reality.

4. The concept of "Samudra Manthan" – churning of knowledge:

The concept of "Samudra Manthan," or the churning of the ocean, serves as a powerful metaphor that encapsulates the nature of seeking, thinking, and the quest for knowledge at the Maha Kumbh. This mythic narrative from Hindu scripture provides a vivid illustration of the struggle to uncover the ultimate truths and highlights the importance of perseverance, collaboration, and a deep commitment to the pursuit of wisdom.

In the story, the gods and demons, recognising their

collective need for the elixir of immortality, decide to work together, using Mount Mandara as a churning rod and the serpent Vasuki as a rope. This cooperative action represents the coming together of diverse perspectives and the recognition that wisdom can be achieved through the efforts of all involved.

The churning process itself is depicted as a long, arduous, and often tumultuous undertaking, representing the challenges and hardships one faces during their quest for knowledge. The initial results of this churning process are not always positive or desirable; in fact, the first things that emerge are poisons, symbolising the difficulties that one faces when embarking on the path of self-discovery. This implies that the process of seeking truth often involves facing uncomfortable realities and challenging aspects of the self. But perseverance eventually leads to the emergence of Amrita, the elixir of immortality, which symbolises ultimate knowledge, liberation, and enlightenment.

The concept of Amrita suggests that through diligent efforts, wisdom and understanding can be achieved. Regarding the Maha Kumbh, we can perceive the "Samudra Manthan" process as the amalgamation of diverse traditions, thoughts, and perspectives. Each group, sect, and individual is like a different ingredient in this process, contributing their own insights and experiences, creating a dynamic and evolving environment.

The spiritual practices, philosophical discussions, and intellectual debates that take place at the Maha Kumbh can all be seen as acts of churning, seeking to sift through different perspectives and come to a deeper understanding.

The "poisons" that emerge may represent uncomfortable truths, challenging beliefs, or the realisation of one's limitations. But with patience, diligence, and perseverance, it is believed that seekers can ultimately reach the "Amrita," the nectar of ultimate wisdom.

The concept of "Samudra Manthan" provides a framework to understand the complexities of seeking knowledge, enlightenment, and truth, and it embodies the spirit of the Maha Kumbh, where individuals unite in this shared endeavour, recognising the power of collective action, perseverance, and commitment to spiritual understanding.

This is not a purely intellectual process; it also involves the engagement of the mind, the heart, and the spirit. Recognising that true knowledge involves both comprehension and personal transformation,

CHAPTER 5: THE KUMBH AS A LIVING LIBRARY: WISDOM, MEDITATION, AND AMPLIFIED PRACTICE

1. The Maha Kumbh as a unique space for observing amplified meditation and spiritual practices:

The Maha Kumbh transcends the typical spiritual gathering to become an unparalleled space for observing meditation and spiritual practices at a scale and intensity not easily found elsewhere. This unique setting offers an extraordinary opportunity to explore the effects of focused intention, spiritual discipline, and collective consciousness on individuals and groups, transforming the Kumbh into a "living laboratory' of meditation.

The very atmosphere at the Maha Kumbh is infused with spiritual energy, stemming from the convergence of millions of seekers, each engaged in various forms of spiritual practice. This collective focus creates a heightened sense of awareness that allows for the amplification of individual practices. This is especially relevant for those who practice meditation, which is a central part of the Hindu tradition.

Meditation and Spiritual Practices

Various types of meditation are practiced at Kumbh, from guided visualisations to quiet contemplation, creating a diverse field of practices that are open to observation. The energetic effects can be amplified by the sheer number of people meditating at the same time. This creates a unique setting for studying consciousness and inner awareness. At the Kumbh, one can find various yoga traditions that involve physical postures, breathing exercises, and meditation, all focused on achieving union with the divine.

The discipline required to participate in these practices creates a fascinating subject of study. One can explore the physiological effects of prolonged yoga practice and the influence of discipline on the practitioner's state of mind. The sheer number of people practicing creates a collective energy that is palpable and worth exploring. The presence of so many spiritual practitioners at the Kumbh also contributes to the amplification of meditation and spiritual practices. The presence of enlightened individuals can serve as an example for others and can also enhance the spiritual environment, inspiring those in attendance. The intense and pervasive presence of meditation and spiritual practice makes the Maha Kumbh a remarkable place for researchers to observe the phenomenon. By studying this phenomenon in its natural setting, we gain insights not found in any lab environment.

This convergence of factors makes the Kumbh a unique living laboratory for research into meditation, c, and collective consciousness.

2. The potential for studying the effects of long-term meditation and spiritual discipline:

The Maha Kumbh provides an exceptional opportunity to study the transformative effects of long-term meditation and spiritual discipline on individuals. Many of those who attend have been practicing these disciplines for many years—some for their entire lives. This makes the Maha Kumbh a unique opportunity for them to observe the long-term effects, which they might not have had the chance to study in the controlled lab setting. These individuals come from diverse backgrounds and practice various forms of meditation, providing a wide spectrum of data for study. Examining these individuals can yield significant understanding of the evolution of consciousness over time.

Psychological Benefits of Meditation

The practice of meditation involves cultivating a state of focused attention and inner awareness. Those who engage in regular practice tend to experience significant changes in their mental states, including reduced stress and anxiety, an increased sense of well-being, and improved ability to focus and concentrate. By studying these transformations over time, researchers can gain a clearer picture of the psychological benefits of meditation. Observing the effects of long-term practice can allow for a more nuanced view of the transformations.

In addition to the psychological benefits, the study of these individuals can provide an insight into the physiological impact of meditation. Regular practice is associated with improved cardiovascular health, reduced blood pressure, and positive changes in the brain, all of which may have implications for wider medical and health concerns. The sustained practice of spiritual disciplines such as yoga and austerity, as practised by many Sadhus at the Kumbh, provides researchers with unique opportunities to study the effects of these practices on the body, mind, and spirit. This observation of these practices also provides invaluable opportunities to study the impact of lifestyle choices on the human experience and may also offer paths to improved quality of life and well-being.

The diversity of meditation styles and spiritual practices that are present at the Kumbh creates an environment where we can study many different approaches and their effects on the practitioner, allowing for the possibility of a more holistic understanding. This long-term observation within the dynamic setting of the Maha Kumbh provides invaluable insights into the ways that focused awareness can contribute to human well-being and spiritual transformation.

3. The unique insights offered by observing the behaviours of enlightened souls at Kumbh:

The Maha Kumbh attracts not just seekers, but also a diverse array of enlightened souls who have dedicated their lives to the pursuit of wisdom and self-realization. These individuals, often referred to as saints, sages, and masters, embody profound levels of spiritual understanding and present a rare opportunity for researchers to observe wisdom and consciousness.

The Maha Kumbh provides a valuable opportunity to examine the characteristics, behaviours, and approaches of these enlightened individuals, yielding unique insights into the nature of higher consciousness. One of the unique aspects of this observation is that it occurs in a natural setting, at the Maha Kumbh, where spiritual practice is amplified. This offers valuable insight compared to observations within a controlled lab environment. The behaviours of these enlightened individuals provide a view into what is possible, inspiring both scientists and lay observers. They often exhibit a deep sense of peace, compassion, and wisdom, indicating the transformative power of spiritual practice.

Studying how they interact with others and how they respond to the large-scale environment of the Maha Kumbh may offer a deeper perspective on human psychology and behaviour. The opportunity to observe and interact with enlightened individuals, including their daily routines, practices, and teachings, allows for an understanding of how they have reached the higher stages of spiritual development. This observation can include the physical, psychological, and emotional impacts of spiritual transformation. These interactions also provide researchers a chance to explore the different methods that are employed by different individuals on the path to enlightenment, each with a unique style and spiritual lineage, providing an opportunity to explore a multitude of approaches to higher consciousness. This observation can include unique approaches to meditation, discipline, and service.

Also, seeing them in the context of the Maha Kumbh and observing how they share wisdom with those who seek it makes this a unique scientific opportunity. This environment offers a platform to learn not only from their words but also from their very presence and embodiment of wisdom. Their behaviour is a reflection of higher awareness, consciousness, and human potential, offering unique insights into our collective nature.

4. The Maha Kumbh as a living repository of wisdom traditions:

The Maha Kumbh transcends its role as a spiritual gathering and emerges as a living repository of ancient wisdom traditions, offering an unparalleled opportunity to study and understand the depth and complexity of India's spiritual heritage. These ancient traditions are not just historical relics; they are living, evolving bodies of knowledge that are embodied by the practices and teachings present at the Kumbh.

The Kumbh is an embodiment of India's rich spiritual traditions, bringing together ancient methods of practice and ways of seeking. This gathering allows for the preservation, transmission, and exploration of these traditions, making the Maha Kumbh a vital centre for spiritual learning. These traditions, including yoga, Vedanta, Ayurveda, and diverse spiritual lineages, are all actively practiced, taught, and shared at the Kumbh. This integration of wisdom traditions makes the Kumbh a living library that is alive and relevant to the modern world.

The diversity of wisdom traditions provides an incredible wealth of information to researchers, and they offer insight into multiple perspectives and approaches to seeking truth and meaning. The Kumbh also allows for exploration of the social, cultural, and historical contexts of these wisdom traditions, seeing them not in isolated locations but in the context of human practice.

The living nature of these traditions is one of the most valuable resources present at the Kumbh. The Maha Kumbh provides a space where knowledge is not confined to books and scriptures but is actively shared through interactions, teachings, and spiritual practices. Through embodied experience and transmission, the traditions remain alive and relevant in the modern world. The traditions themselves are also subject to ongoing interpretations and reinterpretations, evolving as they are passed down from generation to generation. This process of evolution provides a glimpse into the ways that spiritual traditions adapt and change while maintaining their core principles. This means that those studying the traditions at the Kumbh are engaging with something both old and new, an ancient lineage that is also constantly being created.

The gathering together of these living traditions makes the Maha Kumbh a treasure trove of wisdom, where the past, present, and future come together. This allows researchers an unparalleled opportunity to study, learn from, and contribute to the rich spiritual heritage of India.

CHAPTER 6: A SPIRITUAL SPECTACLE: THE SANGAM OF SOULS

1. The Maha Kumbh is the largest spiritual gathering on earth:

The Maha Kumbh undeniably earns its title as the largest spiritual gathering on earth. The sheer scale of the event is unparalleled, drawing millions of pilgrims from across India and all corners of the globe. This convergence of humanity transforms the landscape of Prayagraj into a vibrant and dynamic spectacle, creating an awe-inspiring demonstration of human faith, devotion, and community. The numbers themselves are staggering, with tens of millions of people assembling at the Sangam to bathe in the holy waters, creating a scene that is beyond the scope of everyday human experience. This scale of the human gathering creates a unique environment for scientists to explore crowd dynamics, mass behaviour, and social phenomena, which can help provide valuable insights into social sciences and other related disciplines.

The diversity of individuals is as impressive as the scale itself, as people from all backgrounds, cultures, and social strata come together in one place, setting aside the differences that typically define them and uniting in their shared pursuit of spiritual awakening. The unique nature of the gathering creates a fascinating microcosm of human society, where various cultures are mixed. Due to the size of the gathering, it is a great chance to learn more about the power of collective consciousness by seeing how individual goals affect the environment's overall energetic vibration.

The spiritual intentions of so many people create a palpable energy that is worth exploring from a scientific and spiritual perspective. Also, in addition to this massive congregation of pilgrims, the Maha Kumbh attracts thousands of Sadhus, saints, sages, and masters, which is a rare opportunity to observe so many spiritual teachers and enlightened souls in one place.

The large scale of the event creates a unique platform for cultural exchange, as people share traditions, customs, and perspectives with one another. This exchange not only enriches the individual experiences of those who attend, but it also facilitates a deeper appreciation for the diversity of human expression. The sheer scale of the human gathering, spiritual intention, and cultural diversity make the Maha Kumbh a unique phenomenon worth scientific exploration. The Maha Kumbh offers an unparalleled platform to explore human behaviour on an unprecedented scale.

2. Exploring the significance of the "Sangam" and the convergence of spiritual currents:

The "Sangam," the sacred confluence of the Ganges, Yamuna, and the mythical Saraswati rivers at Prayagraj, is not simply a geographical location; it is a powerful symbol of spiritual convergence and the heart of the Maha Kumbh. The confluence of these three rivers represents more than just the merging of bodies of water; it signifies the union of diverse spiritual currents, traditions, and energies and becomes the focal point of the Maha Kumbh's spiritual significance.

The Ganges, known as "Ganga Ma" or Mother Ganga, is considered the holiest river in Hinduism, associated with purity, life, and the divine. The Yamuna, or "Jamuna Ma," is also considered a sacred river, often connected with love, devotion, and the playful aspects of the divine. These two rivers physically come together in Prayagraj, creating a palpable sense of spiritual presence and a source of purification for all those who immerse themselves in its waters. Also, there is the mythical Saraswati River, which is believed to flow beneath the surface, representing wisdom, knowledge, and creative power. The convergence of these three rivers is believed to amplify their sacred qualities and to create a uniquely potent energy at the Sangam.

The belief is that when the physical waters come together, the spiritual energies that each represents are also combined, creating a location that is capable of providing a path to spiritual awakening. The spiritual significance of the Sangam draws seekers from all walks of life, each seeking a connection with the divine and the blessings of the holy waters.

The experience of bathing at the Sangam transcends mere physical purification; it is also meant to represent an inner cleansing, a renewal of spirit, and a re-connection with one's inner self. The Sangam is seen as a point where the human world intersects with the divine, where seekers may experience deep transformation and insight. The convergence of spiritual currents at the Sangam is not merely a phenomenon that is unique to the Maha Kumbh; it is a universal symbol of union, wholeness, and interconnectedness.

This symbol reminds us that, despite the differences in background and experience, we are all ultimately connected, and we share a common desire to seek truth. For those studying the Kumbh, the Sangam is more than just a location to study; it is a symbol of the transformative potential of spiritual devotion and the deep interconnection of the human spirit.

The Sangam serves as a focal point for the Maha Kumbh and an inspiration for seekers to recognise the unity underlying all diversity.

3. The interplay of Bhakti (devotion) and Gyan (knowledge) traditions:

The Maha Kumbh provides a vibrant display of the interplay between two fundamental pathways of spiritual realisation: Bhakti (devotion) and Gyan (knowledge). These two paths, while distinct in their approaches, are not mutually exclusive. They represent two different ways in which seekers connect with the divine. The coming together of these two approaches makes the Maha Kumbh a vibrant environment for the exploration of spiritual pathways.

Bhakti, the path of devotion, is often expressed through love, service, and surrender to a personal form of the divine. Bhakti traditions involve the use of rituals, prayers, music, and other forms of worship to create a deep and intimate relationship with the divine. For those practicing Bhakti, the goal of spiritual realisation is to experience divine love and surrender completely to the will of God. The practices of Bhakti are accessible to all, regardless of intellectual ability, background, or social standing, and its emphasis on emotion makes it a powerful means for spiritual awakening.

Gyan, or the path of knowledge, emphasises understanding the ultimate nature of reality through study, contemplation, and self-inquiry. The traditions of Gyan often involve rigorous study of sacred scriptures, philosophical analysis, and deep meditation. For those who practice Gyan, the objective is to achieve clarity of mind and understand the true nature of the self. Gyan is not just about gathering information; it also includes personal experience and internal transformation, allowing for a deeper awareness of ultimate reality.

At the Maha Kumbh, these two paths are present side by side, highlighting the different ways in which seekers explore the spiritual realm. Many pilgrims are drawn to Bhakti, expressing their devotion through acts of worship at the Sangam. At the same time, many Sadhus, saints, and masters engage in Gyan traditions, seeking profound wisdom through contemplation and philosophical inquiry.

The interplay between these two traditions reveals that they are not inherently separate but complementary paths that lead to the same destination. Many find that incorporating both Bhakti and Gyan into their practice can enhance their spiritual growth. They realise that love is an important component of knowledge and that knowledge is a path to deepening devotion. The Maha Kumbh provides a unique setting to explore these two paths, allowing seekers to witness both in all their diversity. The Maha Kumbh demonstrates that these two paths provide options for all who seek spiritual insight.

4. The communal environment and its impact on individual seeking:

The communal environment of the Maha Kumbh creates a unique and powerful context for individual spiritual seeking. The shared experience of millions of people coming together, united in their pursuit of spiritual growth, generates a potent collective energy that profoundly influences individual experience.

The environment itself becomes an important factor in one's spiritual journey. Unlike the isolation that many seek in their spiritual practice, the Kumbh creates an environment that is a supportive space for individual seeking. The sheer scale of the event creates a sense of shared purpose, reminding individuals that they are a part of something larger than themselves. This collective feeling of interconnectedness helps to generate a sense of belonging and removes many of the feelings of isolation that may be found in daily life.

Also, the shared rituals, such as bathing at the Sangam, allow for a sense of communal transformation, where each individual feels connected to their community. The intense atmosphere of the Kumbh enhances spiritual practices, and the energy generated from millions of people focused on their spiritual practices helps individuals to delve deeper into their own inner experiences.

Also, the presence of enlightened individuals provides space for learning and creates an environment where individuals are encouraged and inspired to explore their spiritual possibilities. The communal environment also provides a powerful source of social support. Individuals often find themselves engaging in dialogues with like-minded seekers, which often encourages them to reflect on their beliefs and experiences.

The Maha Kumbh allows for interfaith and cross-cultural discussions, creating an environment where people are exposed to diverse viewpoints and thereby increasing their understanding of others. The Maha Kumbh is both a place of individual spiritual seeking and an opportunity for collective growth and transformation. For researchers, it presents a rare opportunity to observe the interplay between individual experiences and the larger social, spiritual, and cultural environments. By understanding how the communal environment influences individual seeking, we may gain deeper insights into the human condition and also the ways that culture affects individual growth.

Ultimately, the Maha Kumbh is more than just a religious event; it is a grand confluence of faith, wisdom, and cultural heritage. It serves as a living testament to the power of collective devotion and the boundless potential of human spirituality.

CHAPTER 7: INDIA: THE LAND OF SEEKERS, NOT BELIEVERS

1. Exploring India as the land of seekers and its contribution to philosophy and spirituality:

India is the land of seekers, exploring its profound contribution to philosophy and spirituality. Entering India—not as a visitor admiring its traditions, but as a seeker on a timeless journey of discovery.This is not just a land of believers, clinging to rigid dogma. It is a land of seekers, individuals driven by an insatiable curiosity to unravel the mysteries of existence. This fundamental difference—seeking over simply believing—is the key to understanding India's extraordinary spiritual and philosophical heritage. It is a land where questioning is not heresy but a sacred act.

Picture ancient sages, their faces etched with wisdom, meditating in Himalayan caves, wrestling with the nature of reality. Wandering ascetics, carrying nothing but a begging bowl, journey across the vast subcontinent, seeking enlightenment through diverse spiritual paths.This spirit of inquiry, this relentless pursuit of truth, is woven into the very fabric of Indian culture. It is not about accepting pre-packaged answers; it is about embarking on a personal journey of self-discovery.

India is not defined by a single, monolithic creed. Instead, it is a vibrant tapestry woven from countless threads of spiritual exploration. A rich tapestry of philosophies, spanning from the ancient wisdom of the Vedas and Upanishads to the refined insights of later schools of thought and the ecstatic expressions of devotional traditions. This landscape is dynamic, constantly evolving, adapting, and responding to the changing times.

India's contribution to the world's spiritual landscape is its unwavering emphasis on individual inquiry. It acknowledges that wisdom is not a universally applicable concept. What resonates with one seeker may not resonate with another. A limitless spiritual mosaic that intertwines diverse paths, practices, and perspectives. Everyone is encouraged to explore, to experiment, and to find the path that speaks to their soul.

This emphasis on seeking has given rise to an astonishing array of spiritual practices. Yogis bend their bodies into intricate postures, their breath flowing in rhythmic harmony, uniting body and mind. Devotees chant ancient mantras, their voices echoing with devotion and longing. Meditators sit in silent stillness, their minds seeking the profound peace within. This rich tapestry of practices embodies India's deep dedication to the individual's spiritual journey.

Rather than providing a single, definitive answer, India's spiritual traditions empower seekers to explore their own questions. It is a recognition that truth is not something to be passively received but something to be actively discovered. A student or devotee sits at the feet of a guru, not merely absorbing wisdom but engaging in vibrant dialogue—questioning, challenging, and ultimately discovering their own understanding. This emphasis on personal responsibility and autonomy is a hallmark of the Indian approach to spirituality.

The Maha Kumbh is a microcosm of this grand tradition of seeking. Envision millions of pilgrims uniting at the sacred river confluence, each pursuing their own profound quest for spiritual fulfillment. It is a gathering of seekers from all walks of life, representing a vast spectrum of beliefs, practices, and traditions. The Kumbh is a living testament to India's inclusive approach to spirituality—embracing diversity and recognising the validity of multiple paths.

India's greatest gift to the world is this very spirit of seeking. It is a recognition that the spiritual journey is not a destination but a lifelong process of exploration, self-reflection, and growth. It is an invitation to question, to learn, to evolve, and to ultimately discover our own unique truth. This emphasis on self-reflection and personal experience is a valuable lesson applicable to all human endeavours, reminding us that the pursuit of knowledge, whether spiritual or scientific, is a journey of continuous discovery.

2. The concept of "Veda Bhoomi," "Karma Bhoomi," and "Deva Bhoomi."

The concepts of Veda Bhoomi, Karma Bhoomi, and Deva Bhoomi come alive, vividly illustrating India's rich and diverse spiritual landscape.

India, known as Veda Bhoomi, the "Land of the Vedas," is where ancient rishis, guided by divine inspiration, composed sacred hymns and profound philosophical insights that became the foundation of Hindu tradition. Envision these verses, not just as words on a page, but as living mantras, resonating with cosmic energy. The Vedas, with their rich tapestry of knowledge, from cosmology to rituals to the nature of consciousness, are India's invaluable gift to the world, a testament to its ancient wisdom. Veda Bhoomi represents India as the cradle of spiritual knowledge, a land where profound truths were discovered and codified and where this wisdom continues to be passed down through generations. It is a land where the echoes of ancient chants still reverberate, connecting seekers to the wisdom of the ages.

India is Karma Bhoomi, the "Land of Action." Picture individuals, not just contemplating the divine, but actively engaging with the world, fulfilling their dharma, their righteous duty. The concept of karma, the principle of cause and effect, permeates every aspect of life. Every action, thought, and intention has consequences, shaping one's destiny. Karma Bhoomi emphasises that spirituality is not passive; It is a call to action, a recognition that each individual has a role to play in the grand scheme of things. It is a place where people put spiritual principles into practice, expressing their faith through action and service. Tilling the soil by farmers, merchants conducting business with integrity, and families upholding their traditions—each action, a form of karma, contributes to the cosmic balance.

India is also called Deva Bhoomi, the "Land of the Gods." It is a landscape dotted with temples, sacred rivers, and pilgrimage sites, each imbued with divine presence. Gods and goddesses are not distant figures but active participants in the lives of devotees, their stories woven into the fabric of everyday life. Deva Bhoomi is a land where the divine is not abstract but palpable, where the boundaries between the sacred and the mundane blur. It is a land where devotion is expressed in countless ways, from elaborate rituals to simple acts of kindness. Pilgrim's bathing in the Ganges, their prayers carried by the flowing water, or devotees offering flowers and incense to their chosen deity, their hearts filled with love and reverence.

The intertwining of these three concepts, Veda Bhoomi, Karma Bhoomi, and Deva Bhoomi, forms a complete picture of India's spiritual landscape. It is a place where transcendent wisdom meets active engagement with the world, where the divine is both transcendent and immanent. It is a land that invites exploration, growth, and a deep connection to the sacred. These ideas transform the landscape from simply a geographic location to a powerful spiritual symbol, underscoring India's role as a place of spiritual awakening for the individual and humanity. It is a land where the past, present, and future intertwine, creating a timeless tapestry of spiritual seeking and divine grace.

3. Seeking and Scientific Inquiry: Two Sides of the Same Coin: Delving Deeper

Vedanta plays a crucial role in bridging wisdom and inquiry, shaping the deep interplay between spiritual pursuit and scientific exploration in India. In India, seeking and scientific inquiry are not viewed as opposing forces, but rather as complementary paths to understanding reality. Scientists meticulously conduct experiments in a lab, driven by a burning curiosity to unravel the mysteries of the universe. Yogis meditate in a secluded cave, delving deep into the recesses of their consciousness, seeking the ultimate truth of existence. Both are driven by the same fundamental impulse: the desire to understand, to explore, and to uncover the hidden workings of reality.

In contrast to certain cultures that frequently perceive science and spirituality as opposing worldviews, India's tradition acknowledges the intrinsic interconnection between the two. Both emphasise the importance of inquiry, questioning, and personal exploration. The scientist formulates hypotheses, designs experiments, and analyses data, constantly questioning established theories and seeking new insights. The spiritual seeker engages in self-reflection, contemplates philosophical questions, and explores various spiritual practices, constantly questioning their own assumptions and seeking deeper understanding.

Ancient Indian scholars were not only deep thinkers pondering philosophical questions but also pioneers making groundbreaking advancements in mathematics, astronomy, and medicine. Aryabhata, for example, revolutionised astronomy with his accurate calculations of planetary movements, whereas Sushruta, the father of surgery, performed complex surgical procedures centuries before modern medicine. These ancient scientists were not just accumulating knowledge; they were seeking to understand the underlying principles that govern the universe, often integrating their scientific insights with their philosophical and spiritual beliefs.

The goal of seeking in the Indian context extends beyond mere information gathering; it encompasses personal transformation. The seeker is not just trying to understand the world; they are also striving to transform themselves, to achieve a deeper understanding of their own nature and their place in the cosmos. This emphasis on personal experience is also a crucial aspect of India's scientific tradition. Just as scientists rely on empirical evidence to validate their theories, spiritual seekers emphasise direct experience as the ultimate source of truth.

The Maha Kumbh itself is a powerful example of this integration between seeking and scientific inquiry. Researchers have the opportunity to explore how large gatherings shape human behavior, delving into the psychological impacts of spiritual discipline and the physiological transformations induced by meditation. The Kumbh becomes a living laboratory, a place where the scientific and the spiritual intersect, offering unique opportunities to study the complex interplay between consciousness, culture, and human experience.

4. Vedanta: A Framework for Seeking and Research:

Vedanta, the philosophical culmination of the Vedas, provides a profound framework for both spiritual seeking and scientific research in the Indian context. It offers a comprehensive understanding of reality, consciousness, and the relationship between the individual and the universe, providing a foundation for both inner and outer exploration.

Vedanta stands as a grand intellectual legacy, forged through centuries of deep philosophical inquiry and spiritual enlightenment. The principle of non-duality, which is at the heart of it, says that the ultimate reality (Brahman) is one and that everything, including the individual self, is a manifestation of this oneness. This radical idea has profound implications for understanding the nature of reality, consciousness, and human potential.

Vedanta, with its diverse schools of thought, encourages inquiry, critical thinking, and questioning. It is not about blind faith but about intellectual and experiential exploration. The Upanishads, the core texts of Vedanta, are filled with dialogues, debates, and profound insights into the nature of existence. They invite seekers to question everything—to delve deep into the mysteries of life and death.

Vedanta also emphasises self-knowledge as the ultimate goal. It encourages introspection, self-reflection, and the exploration of one's own consciousness. This emphasis on inner awareness aligns with the scientific approach, which also acknowledges the importance of observation and experience. Vedanta, therefore, provides a bridge between inner and outer exploration, between subjective experience and objective inquiry.

For scientific research, Vedanta offers valuable insights into the nature of reality, human consciousness, and ethics. Its emphasis on non-duality can inform our understanding of the interconnectedness of all things, from the subatomic realm to the vastness of the cosmos. Its exploration of consciousness can provide new perspectives on the mind-body problem and the nature of subjective experience. And its ethical principles, rooted in compassion and non-violence, can guide scientific research towards socially beneficial and morally responsible outcomes.

Vedanta, therefore, is not just a philosophical tradition; it is a framework for integrating scientific understanding with spiritual insights, a guide for exploring the fundamental questions that have preoccupied humanity for millennia. It recognises that both scientific inquiry and spiritual inquiry are part of the same journey—a quest to uncover the deepest truths about the cosmos and our place within it.

CHAPTER 8: MEETING THE ENLIGHTENED: RARE ENCOUNTERS AND UNPARALLELED LEARNING

1. The opportunity to learn directly from enlightened individuals and their years of dedicated practice:

The Maha Kumbh offers an extraordinary opportunity to learn directly from enlightened individuals who have dedicated their lives to spiritual practice and self-realisation. This provides seekers with a rare chance to connect with those who have attained profound levels of wisdom and understanding, learning directly from their lived experiences. This direct learning experience transcends the limitations of theory and books, allowing for an embodied transmission of wisdom that cannot be found elsewhere.

The unique atmosphere at the Kumbh provides an opportunity for personal interaction and dialogue, which may often be spontaneous, direct, and transformative. The presence of these enlightened individuals enriches the spiritual energy of the Kumbh, and the teachings are often tailored to the specific needs and questions of those who approach them. Many of these masters have spent decades or even lifetimes in dedicated practice, often living in seclusion, immersing themselves in meditation, study, and contemplation. Their lives provide a living example of the potential of spiritual transformation. Their experiences, insights, and teaching offer a guide on the path to self-discovery and provide a valuable resource for learning and growth. This learning comes not only from the words of these masters but from their very being, which often exudes a unique energy and perspective.

The opportunity to observe and listen to these individuals provides a glimpse into the higher states of consciousness. The interactions are not limited to formal teaching; they also come through informal conversations, shared meals, and the shared experience of participation in the Kumbh. These encounters underscore the significance of human connection in the learning process, emphasising the sharing of true wisdom through relationships. For researchers, the opportunity to observe and document this phenomenon is extremely important.

The unique opportunity to access and learn from these rare and unique individuals is one of the most valuable assets of the Maha Kumbh.

2. Insights gained from observing and engaging with individuals from diverse spiritual backgrounds:

The Maha Kumbh is not only a gathering of enlightened individuals but also a meeting point for those from diverse spiritual backgrounds, each with a unique set of beliefs, practices, and traditions. This rich diversity offers invaluable learning opportunities for those interested in both the science and spirit of seeking. Observing and engaging with individuals from diverse spiritual backgrounds allows for a deeper understanding of the multiplicity of pathways that exist, with each representing a valid approach to spirituality. The Maha Kumbh is a place where all of these traditions can come together.

The interaction with individuals from diverse spiritual backgrounds also helps to overcome preconceived notions and biases, expanding the understanding of the nature of human experience and creating greater inclusivity. The opportunity to hear personal stories and perspectives often results in a deeper appreciation of the diversity of approaches to spiritual development. By understanding a multitude of beliefs, practices, and cultural traditions, the seeker begins to expand their own understanding of reality. Observing individuals from various spiritual backgrounds also provides opportunities to understand the commonalities between these traditions.

The Maha Kumbh highlights that, despite the diverse perspectives, there is often a shared understanding of basic human values and spiritual goals, fostering a sense of unity in the quest for spiritual awakening. This convergence offers the chance to comprehend the fundamental principles and similarities shared by various approaches. Through observation and participation, seekers are challenged to broaden their understanding of the world and recognise the multitude of pathways for spiritual realisation.

Each perspective contributes to a comprehensive understanding of consciousness and the nature of reality. The exchange of ideas, stories, and experiences is a significant component of the learning that takes place at the Kumbh. This creates an invaluable space for inter-spiritual dialogue, promoting greater tolerance, compassion, and understanding of the human journey.

The Maha Kumbh emphasises the importance of respecting the diverse traditions that exist and learning from each inclusively and openly.

3. The unique experience of interacting with wisdom holders:

The experience of interacting with wisdom holders at the Maha Kumbh is unlike any other, offering profound opportunities for learning, inspiration, and personal transformation. These interactions go beyond intellectual learning and create a unique opportunity to understand wisdom on an experiential and embodied level. These wisdom holders, who may include saints, sages, masters, and enlightened teachers, possess unique levels of insight, often stemming from years of dedicated practice and deep contemplation. They embody a unique blend of intellect and intuition, often providing guidance that goes beyond the limitations of ordinary experience.

The wisdom that they share is not simply based on knowledge learnt from books but also on their own lives and experiences, which gives their guidance authenticity and resonance. Interactions with these individuals often take place in informal settings, as they are offered direct teaching and may also provide personal guidance and individualised wisdom to those who seek it. These informal settings can often feel transformative and profound, leaving a lasting impression that is impossible to experience elsewhere. The very presence of these wisdom holders can often be transforming and inspirational, and there is often a unique energy that is both calming and uplifting.

Simply by being in the presence of these enlightened individuals, many seekers find themselves transformed. The unique experience of interacting with these wisdom holders provides more than just learning; it is also an opportunity to understand the possibilities of human potential and the impact of spiritual practice on life. It also serves as an example of how we might be able to live more authentic and meaningful lives. The interactions can also catalyze personal transformation, prompting individuals to reassess their own beliefs, values, and paths of seeking.

The guidance offered is specific and practical, often addressing the deeper questions of the heart and providing insights that may provide direction in times of confusion and uncertainty. The interactions provide a profound experience of wisdom and compassion. These wisdom holders are a precious gift to the Maha Kumbh, making it such a powerful and valuable location for those seeking enlightenment. The experience of interacting with them provides inspiration and guidance for years to come.

4. The direct transmission of knowledge and experience:

The Maha Kumbh underscores the immense value of the direct transmission of knowledge and experience, highlighting that wisdom is not simply acquired through books or lectures; it is best transmitted through personal interactions, observation, and shared experiences. Direct transmission is the embodied passing of knowledge, wisdom, and spiritual energy from one person to another, often done through informal interactions, shared practices, and personal guidance. This approach to learning recognises that true knowledge is more than just intellectual understanding; it also involves integration with the heart and spirit.

At the Maha Kumbh, direct transmission of knowledge is particularly important because it ensures that ancient spiritual traditions and practices are not just preserved but also kept relevant and alive for future generations. The presence of living wisdom holders creates an environment where individuals can be immersed in the authentic practices of different traditions.

The direct transmission of wisdom goes beyond the words that are shared; it often involves the subtle transfer of energy and consciousness between the teacher and the student. This type of connection often creates an environment for a deeper and more transformative learning experience. This transmission often takes place in informal settings, such as shared meals, spontaneous conversations, and participation in rituals, allowing a unique environment of learning. Through observation of the daily lives of enlightened beings, one can gain an understanding of their wisdom and the subtle qualities of presence that they often embody.

Direct experience, such as participating in spiritual practices like bathing at the Sangam, is an important part of this learning, and these unique experiences can offer an individual a chance for personal transformation and a greater understanding of their own nature. In the present day of information overload, the value of direct transmission is more important than ever.

The Maha Kumbh provides an important reminder that true knowledge requires heart, intention, and genuine human connection. The value of direct experience also provides scientists and researchers with a way to see how spiritual traditions and practices can be passed from generation to generation, as well as to observe human transformation.

The Maha Kumbh provides a living example of the impact of shared experiences and is an essential part of the learning experience that is found at this unique event.

CHAPTER 9: MAHA KUMBH: A HEAVEN FOR SCIENTISTS AND RESEARCH

1. The Science Behind Maha Kumbh Mela

The Kumbh Mela, a mesmerising display of faith and devotion, draws millions of pilgrims to India's sacred waterways. It is more than just a religious gathering; It is a heavenly event steeped in ancient wisdom, combining science and spirituality. This chapter goes into the science of this exceptional celebration, looking at astronomical calculations, water purification procedures, crowd management strategies, and health practices that contribute to the Kumbh Mela's status as a marvel of human ingenuity and cultural heritage.

Significance of Kumbh Mela

The Kumbh Mela, which means "festival of the sacred pitcher," has its roots in Hindu mythology and is based on the legend of the Samudra Manthan, the churning of the cosmic ocean. According to this old legend, gods and devils fought for Amrit, the nectar of immortality. During this cosmic conflict, drips of the elixir fell on Earth in four locations: Prayagraj, Haridwar, Ujjain, and Nashik. The touch of Amrit sanctified these locations, making them hallowed venues for the Kumbh Mela, held on a rotational basis.

Kumbh Mela is an important event in the Hindu calendar, attracting millions of followers seeking spiritual cleansing and emancipation. Pilgrims believe that by immersing themselves in the sacred rivers at these chosen spots, they can wash their souls of impurities and sins, resulting in moksha, or escape from the cycle of birth and death. The festival is more than just a religious rite; It is a profound experience that incorporates astronomy, astrology, spirituality, and a diverse set of social and cultural conventions and activities. It has a "mesmeric influence on ordinary Indians," bringing them together in a common quest for spiritual growth and rebirth.

Astronomical and astrological calculations

Every 12 years, the Sun, Moon, and Jupiter's celestial positions closely coincide with the Kumbh Mela. This time is not accidental; it reflects the ancient wisdom and scientific knowledge that support this enormous festival. When Jupiter enters Aquarius (Kumbh Rashi), and the Sun and Moon coincide in certain positions, the Kumbh Mela begins. People believe that this celestial alignment creates a spiritually charged environment that amplifies the benefits of the holy bath.

Jupiter's influence:

Jupiter, the largest planet in our solar system, takes around 12 years to complete its orbit around the Sun. Jupiter is known in Hindu astrology as Brihaspati, or the guru of the gods, and its location is critical in deciding the timing of the Kumbh Mela. When Jupiter enters Aquarius, it is thought to provide particular energy, making the time ideal for spiritual cleaning and rejuvenation. This convergence with Jupiter's cycle highlights the Kumbh Mela's deep connection to cosmic rhythms.

Sun and Moon's Role:

The Sun and Moon play important roles in the astrological computations for the Kumbh Mela. The Sun's position frequently signals the change of seasons, filling the event with vibrancy and freshness. The Moon's function, especially during Amavasya (New Moon) and Purnima (Full Moon), strengthens the festival's energetic power by leading rituals and pilgrimages.

Water quality and purification methods

With millions of pilgrims immersing themselves in the sacred rivers, protecting water purity during the Kumbh Mela is critical. Authorities use a multipronged approach to ensure pilgrim safety while minimising environmental harm.

Monitoring of the water quality:

Some systems check the quality of water in real time. These systems look at things like faecal coliform levels and biological oxygen demand (BOD). The BOD shows how much oxygen is needed to break down organic matter in water. These technologies assist authorities in assessing water quality and taking appropriate measures to keep it within acceptable levels. Despite these efforts, untreated sewage persists, raising concerns about its potential impact on the river environment.

Sewage Treatment Plants:

To handle the large volumes of sewage created during the festival, temporary Sewage Treatment Plants (STPs) are erected. These STPs process human waste and greywater with modern technologies, guaranteeing that only clean water is released into the environment.

Innovative solutions:

In addition to STPs, a variety of innovative solutions are used to filter water and manage waste. This includes: ISRO and BARC developed the Hybrid Granular Sequencing Batch Reactor (HGSBR) technology, which efficiently cleanses sewage and promotes environmental cleanliness. This demonstrates India's technological breakthroughs in organising large events while minimising environmental damage.

Geotube Technology: Containing and Treating Liquid Waste:

Geotube technology offers an effective solution for dewatering and treating liquid waste generated at the Kumbh Mela. Massive cylindrical geotextile tubes, strategically positioned along the riverbanks, serve as temporary containment systems for wastewater management. These tubes are made of a permeable fabric that allows water to pass through while retaining solid waste particles. The wastewater is pumped into the geotubes, where it undergoes a process of dewatering and filtration. Gravity and natural evaporation help remove excess water, leaving behind concentrated sludge. This sludge can then be further treated or disposed of safely, preventing it from contaminating the rivers.

Geotube technology offers several advantages:

i. *Efficient Dewatering:* Geotubes efficiently remove excess water from wastewater, reducing its volume and making it easier to handle and transport.

ii. *Cost-Effective:* Geotubes are a cost-effective solution compared to traditional wastewater treatment methods, especially for temporary events like the Kumbh Mela.

iii. *Environmentally friendly*: Geotubes minimise the environmental impact of wastewater by preventing it from directly entering rivers and contaminating water.

iv. *Versatile:* Geotubes can be used to treat a variety of liquid waste, such as sewage, industrial wastewater, and contaminated runoff.

Bioremediation: Harnessing the Power of Nature:

Bioremediation is a natural and sustainable approach to cleaning up contaminated water and soil. It uses microorganisms, such as bacteria and fungi, to break pollutants down into harmless substances. These microorganisms are naturally present in the environment and can be further enhanced through specific bioremediation techniques.

At the Kumbh Mela, bioremediation is used to treat wastewater and contaminated soil, reducing dependence on chemical treatments and minimising environmental impact. Bioremediation systems can be set up near the riverbanks or in designated treatment areas. These systems typically involve introducing specific microorganisms or creating conditions that promote the growth of naturally occurring microbes that can break down pollutants.

Bioremediation offers several benefits:

i. *Natural and sustainable*: Bioremediation is a natural and sustainable process that utilises the inherent capabilities of microorganisms to break down pollutants.

ii. *Environmentally friendly:* Bioremediation avoids the use of harsh chemicals and minimises the environmental impact of waste treatment.

iii. *Cost-Effective:* Bioremediation can be a cost-effective solution compared to traditional treatment methods, especially for large-scale events like the Kumbh Mela.

iv. *Versatile:* Bioremediation can be used to treat a variety of pollutants, including organic matter, heavy metals, and pesticides.

A Combined Approach for Environmental Sustainability

Geotube technology and bioremediation are often used in combination to create a comprehensive and sustainable approach to waste management and environmental protection at the Kumbh Mela. Geotubes can be used to dewater and concentrate liquid waste, making it easier for microorganisms to break down pollutants through bioremediation. This combined approach maximises the efficiency of both technologies and minimises the environmental impact of the festival.

The use of geotube technology and bioremediation at the Kumbh Mela demonstrates a commitment to environmental sustainability and a willingness to embrace innovative solutions to address the challenges of waste management. These technologies help protect the sacred rivers, ensure the health and well-being of the pilgrims, and contribute to a cleaner and healthier environment for all.

Crowd Management and Sanitation Techniques

Managing vast crowds at the Kumbh Mela, one of the world's greatest gatherings, is a tremendous effort. The authorities use a blend of ancient and modern approaches to protect the pilgrims' safety and well-being.

AI-Powered Surveillance:

AI-powered cameras and drones perform real-time crowd monitoring and surveillance. These tools assist authorities in monitoring crowd density, predicting probable congestion points, and preventing stampedes. This data-driven crowd control strategy enables preventive interventions while also improving overall event safety.

Integrated Command and Control Centre (ICCC):

The Integrated Command and Control Centre (ICCC) is responsible for crowd management, monitoring, and security at the Kumbh Mela. This centralised centre monitors the entry of devotees, improves communication and coordination among stakeholders, and aids in the prevention of potential hazards, such as overcrowding and stampedes.

Strategic zoning:

The Mela area is segmented into separate zones for entry, congregation, bathing, and exit to facilitate movement and prevent overcrowding. Emergency evacuation zones are constructed to ensure prompt reaction to unforeseen catastrophes. This planned zoning, when combined with AI-powered surveillance, results in a full crowd management system.

RFID Tagging:

The Kumbh Mela uses Radio Frequency Identification (RFID) tagging to locate lost people. This technology assists in reuniting lost individuals with their family and friends, providing an additional degree of protection and security to the event.

Sanitation Measures

The Maha Kumbh Mela, with its massive influx of pilgrims, presents a monumental challenge for sanitation and hygiene. Maintaining a clean and healthy environment for millions of people living in temporary conditions requires meticulous planning and extensive sanitation measures. The authorities responsible for organising the Kumbh Mela have implemented a comprehensive sanitation strategy that combines traditional practices with modern technologies to ensure pilgrims' well-being and protect the environment.

Deployment of Cleaning Workers: An Army of Sanitation:

A dedicated force of sanitation workers, dressed in bright uniforms, tirelessly ensures the cleanliness of the Kumbh Mela. These dedicated individuals are deployed throughout the festival grounds, sweeping streets, collecting garbage, and cleaning toilets and bathing areas. Their tireless efforts ensure that the temporary city stays clean and hygienic, even with the constant influx of pilgrims. Their efforts are crucial in preventing the spread of diseases and maintaining a healthy environment for all.

Numerous Toilets and Urinals: Meeting Basic Needs:

Access to adequate sanitation facilities is essential for maintaining hygiene and preventing the spread of diseases, especially in a massive gathering like the Kumbh Mela. Authorities have installed numerous toilets and urinals throughout the festival grounds, catering to the diverse needs of the pilgrims.

The numerous toilets and urinal facilities include:

i. *"Flag Area" Toilets:* These are designated toilet areas marked with flags, providing easily accessible and visible sanitation facilities for the pilgrims.

ii. *Wayside Urinals:* These are strategically placed urinals along the roads and pathways, offering convenient sanitation options for pilgrims on the move.

iii. *Pit toilets:* These are simple and cost-effective toilets that are suitable for temporary events like the Kumbh Mela.

iv. *PRAI Latrines*: The Planning, Research and Action Institute (PRAI) are improved pit latrines that offer better hygiene and odour control than traditional pit toilets.

The availability of diverse toilet options ensures that pilgrims have access to appropriate sanitation facilities, regardless of their needs or preferences.

Sectional Vehicles and Jet Spray Cleaning Equipment: Modern Sanitation:

Modern sanitation technologies are employed to enhance the efficiency and effectiveness of cleaning operations at the Kumbh Mela. Sectional vehicles, equipped with high-pressure water jets, are used to clean streets, bathing areas, and other public spaces. These vehicles can quickly and effectively remove dirt, debris, and other waste materials, ensuring a clean and hygienic environment for the pilgrims.

Dustbins with Liner Bags: Promoting Waste Segregation:

The festival grounds strategically place dustbins with liner bags to encourage proper waste disposal and segregation. Pilgrims are encouraged to dispose of their waste responsibly, separating recyclable materials from non-recyclable waste. This waste segregation initiative helps reduce the environmental impact of the festival and promotes recycling and resource recovery.

Regular Refilling and Maintenance: Ensuring Continuous Hygiene:

The Kumbh Mela regularly maintains and replenishes its sanitation facilities and equipment to ensure continuous hygiene. The cleaning workers regularly empty dustbins, clean toilets, and replenish supplies. This proactive approach to sanitation maintenance ensures that the facilities remain clean and functional throughout the festival, providing a healthy and hygienic environment for the pilgrims.

A Comprehensive Sanitation Strategy:

The sanitation measures implemented at the Kumbh Mela reflect a comprehensive and multi-faceted approach to hygiene and waste management. By combining traditional practices with modern technologies, the authorities responsible for organising the festival have created a clean, sanitary environment for millions of attendees. These efforts not only protect the health and well-being of the pilgrims but also demonstrate a commitment to environmental sustainability and responsible waste management. The Kumbh Mela serves as a model for large-scale events, showcasing effective sanitation strategies that can be implemented to ensure the health and hygiene of massive gatherings while minimising their environmental impact.

It is important to follow health and hygiene practices

The Kumbh Mela, with its enormous numbers and temporary living circumstances, may pose health risks, including the spread of infectious diseases like influenza and gastroenteritis. However, the authorities implement several health and hygiene precautions to mitigate these hazards and enhance the pilgrims' well-being.

Vaccines and medications:

It is recommended that pilgrims stay up-to-date on basic vaccinations and prescriptions. Healthcare providers provide information about pre-travel vaccines and drugs particular to India.

Food and water safety:

Emphasis is also placed on food and water safety, along with fundamental hand hygiene. Pilgrims are urged to drink only purified or boiling water and eat food from reputable sources.

Health Monitoring and Emergency Preparedness:

Medical camps and rapid reaction teams are deployed to address health emergencies. The pilgrims are encouraged to watch for signs of illness and seek medical assistance if necessary.

Health Benefits:

Beyond addressing potential health risks, the Kumbh Mela encourages a variety of health-promoting actions. The holiday promotes preventive health activities such as fasting and meditation, which are thought to renew the body and mind. These traditions are consistent with modern wellness trends, highlighting the Kumbh Mela's holistic dedication to health and well-being.

Astrological remedies

The Kumbh Mela also includes astrological remedies for treating planetary doshas, which are imbalances caused by unfavourable planetary placements. These cures include rituals like bathing in sacred rivers at specified times, singing mantras, and making offerings. This unique blend of astrological and wellness practices enhances the Kumbh Mela's focus on overall well-being.

Environmental impact and mitigation efforts

The huge scale of the Kumbh Mela has an unavoidable environmental impact. However, substantial efforts are underway to reduce these effects and improve sustainability. The Kumbh Mela has become a prominent advocate for sustainable infrastructure and construction, showcasing its commitment to environmental stewardship.

Eco-friendly practices

The adoption of environmentally friendly materials and

construction procedures is a top priority for organisers. Organisers create temporary structures with sustainability in mind, utilising biodegradable materials where feasible. Initiatives such as the "One Plate, One Bag" campaign encourage the usage of reusable utensils and cloth bags to help reduce plastic waste.

Waste Management

Comprehensive waste management strategies are implemented, incorporating recycling and efficient garbage disposal. Waste segregation practices are carried out to minimize environmental impact and enhance cleanliness.

Water conservation initiatives promote responsible usage and reduce pollution, with pilgrims encouraged to use water mindfully.

Infrastructure is integrating renewable energy, including solar electricity. Energy-efficient lighting and environmentally friendly technology are used.

Afforestation programs aim to mitigate environmental impacts. Planting trees and establishing green spaces help maintain the overall ecological balance. Afforestation programs are undertaken well in advance at Kumbh Mela.

Location-Specific Concerns

The Kumbh Mela's environmental impact varies according to its location. For example, the largest Kumbh Mela, Prayagraj, has the most potential for waste creation and water pollution due to the confluence of rivers and the sheer number of pilgrims. These site-specific difficulties necessitate targeted mitigating strategies to safeguard the environment.

The Kumbh Mela demonstrates the eternal force of faith and the creativity of humans. It is a celebration where science and spirituality meet, and ancient wisdom informs contemporary actions. The Kumbh Mela exemplifies a harmonious blend of tradition and technology, including astronomical calculations, water purification procedures, crowd management tactics, health and hygiene measures, and environmental mitigation efforts. This magnificent festival not only offers a venue for spiritual cleansing and regeneration, but it also acts as a model for sustainable and conscientious event management.

The Kumbh Mela is a remarkable event that effortlessly combines old traditions with modern innovations. It is time, determined by exact astronomical calculations, that demonstrates a thorough comprehension of the universe. The festival's emphasis on purifying goes beyond the spiritual world to include water purification and sanitary procedures that safeguard both pilgrims and the environment. Innovative technology, like AI-powered monitoring and RFID tagging, is used to control large crowds and assure safety. Health practices, ranging from vaccinations to astrology, improve overall well-being. Kumbh Mela also works to reduce its environmental impacts by implementing eco-friendly infrastructure, trash management, and renewable energy programs. The Kumbh Mela is a really amazing celebration of human creativity and cultural history, thanks to its remarkable combination of science and spirituality.

2. Why the Maha Kumbh is a unique site for scientific exploration:

The Maha Kumbh is more than a spiritual gathering; it is a unique and unparalleled site for scientific exploration, offering an environment that is unmatched in its scale, diversity, and complexity. It presents a rare opportunity to study human behaviour, social dynamics, and consciousness on a huge scale. This offers a unique opportunity for the scientific community to expand their understanding of the human experience.

The convergence of millions of people from diverse backgrounds and traditions creates a natural laboratory for observing human behaviour under unique circumstances. This allows us to explore collective consciousness, cultural dynamics, and the effects of shared beliefs on individual actions. The sheer number of individuals, combined with an intense spiritual environment, offers a unique opportunity to explore group dynamics, crowd behaviour, and the spread of ideas in real time. These are all areas that provide rich data for scientists to study the human condition. The intensity of spiritual practices at the Kumbh provides a unique opportunity to study the long-term effects of meditation, discipline, and contemplation. Many of the individuals have dedicated their lives to these spiritual paths, providing a valuable perspective for studying the long-term impact of these practices on their minds, bodies, and spirits.

The Kumbh also provides a unique context for observing the interplay of human beings and their environment, which is crucial for understanding the impact of large human gatherings on the surrounding ecosystem. This provides a unique perspective on human impacts and their interaction with the natural world. This unique event is also a location where we can observe the complexities of human life, from the most extreme forms of asceticism to the daily routines of millions of pilgrims.

The Maha Kumbh stands out from traditional scientific environments because it offers a chance to study human phenomena in a natural, unconstrained setting. The Maha Kumbh offers a profound potential for scientific exploration, providing a platform for new scientific discoveries and insights.

3. Emphasising the living laboratory aspect

The Maha Kumbh must be understood as a "living laboratory," a dynamic and evolving ecosystem that offers unique opportunities for scientific research. The concept of a living laboratory is essential for understanding the value of the Maha Kumbh as a site for research and transforms this event from a cultural event into a valuable scientific resource. This approach shifts away from a controlled setting to allow for observation of real-time human interaction.

The Maha Kumbh is not a static environment; it is dynamic, constantly changing, and influenced by the actions of all those who participate. This makes it a space where researchers can observe processes, human behaviours, and phenomena as they unfold. The Maha Kumbh offers a unique opportunity to study human interaction in a natural, unconstrained setting, allowing researchers to capture the complexities of human experience. The Maha Kumbh is not designed for research, which makes it that much more valuable for scientists to observe how systems develop over time.

The dynamic nature of Kumbh provides opportunities to study how human behaviour adapts to changing circumstances and how different groups interact with each other in a large-scale setting. The scale of the Maha Kumbh makes it such a useful resource for study. The massive nature of the gathering allows for data collection that is impossible anywhere else. This massive gathering provides opportunities to observe behaviours, reactions, and interactions that occur on a large scale. This diversity of participants in the Kumbh provides researchers with an opportunity to study how different groups interact and also allows for a more comprehensive understanding of the human experience as a whole.

The living laboratory perspective allows for observation of the interplay of these complex factors. The Maha Kumbh offers an opportunity to study complex human phenomena in their natural habitat, recognising that human behaviour and experience are shaped by a multitude of interconnected factors and not in a constrained laboratory environment. This living laboratory aspect transforms the Maha Kumbh into an incredibly valuable resource for scientific research, offering a chance for scientific insights that cannot be found anywhere else.

4. Specific scientific fields that could benefit from research in this environment:

The Maha Kumbh provides a fertile ground for scientific exploration across numerous disciplines, offering a unique opportunity for researchers to gain valuable insights into a diverse range of phenomena. This provides a list of opportunities for scientists who are interested in working with the unique setting.

The field of sociology stands to gain important information by studying the complex social interactions of diverse groups within this space. By observing social dynamics, cultural exchanges, and the formation of communities in this setting, sociologists can gain a greater understanding of human behaviour among large populations.

Psychology is another area that would greatly benefit from the Maha Kumbh, providing unique opportunities for the study of consciousness, cognition, and emotional states. The intensity of spiritual practice within the Kumbh provides a unique lens for studying altered states of consciousness, which offers an opportunity to look at the effects of prolonged meditation, discipline, and contemplation on the human mind.

Epidemiological studies also have the opportunity to observe the patterns of disease spread within large populations, which helps gather a comprehensive understanding of the dynamics of infectious diseases.

Environmental science could also explore the effects of the large gathering on the local environment, offering insight into the sustainability and environmental practices that can minimise human impact on the environment.

In addition to the above fields, physics also may find applications at the Maha Kumbh. Research into the collective consciousness and spiritual practices may provide insights into the fundamental nature of the universe and offer a unique opportunity to study interconnectedness.

The Maha Kumbh presents an opportunity to integrate multiple areas of scientific exploration, which offers a more comprehensive view of the human experience and promotes a holistic research approach, allowing insights from different fields to be applied to each other. The Maha Kumbh's potential is limitless.

5. The need for scientists to embrace this opportunity

There is a crucial need for scientists from diverse fields to embrace the unique research opportunities offered by the Maha Kumbh. The scientific community must acknowledge the immense value of this event and actively pursue collaborations that can lead to new scientific insights. The call to action acknowledges the importance of making use of this valuable scientific resource, which is rarely available. The scientific community needs to recognise that this event provides a platform for scientific investigations.

Scientific studies can be used to explore consciousness, group behaviour, the impacts of spiritual practices, and many other areas of research. By embracing the Maha Kumbh as a site of scientific discovery, our scientific and intellectual possibilities are being broadened.Interdisciplinary collaboration is essential to address complex issues, with each field contributing its unique expertise and perspective to allow for scientific collaboration that is both comprehensive and powerful.

Scientists must actively seek collaborations with other

researchers to maximise the benefits of this rare opportunity. Also, research ethics are of utmost importance, and we must approach research with the utmost respect for the spiritual and cultural significance of the Kumbh, acknowledging that the primary focus of the event is spiritual and not scientific. Scientists also have a responsibility to communicate their findings in an accessible manner to benefit society at large and to make information available to communities.

The scientific community must embrace the Maha Kumbh and acknowledge the rare opportunity that it presents, which can lead to scientific advances that also contribute to a greater understanding of humanity, making the research both informative and transformative.

CHAPTER 10: EXPERIMENTS IN PRAYAGRAJ: POTENTIAL FOR FUTURE RESEARCH

1. Specific research areas at Kumbh include psychology, sociology, public health, environmental science, and physics, along with their respective applications

The Maha Kumbh offers fertile ground for research across diverse scientific disciplines, each with unique opportunities for exploration. This chapter explores how different fields can be applied to the unique setting of the Kumbh, highlighting its relevance for research and scientific study.

In the field of psychology, the Maha Kumbh offers unique opportunities to study consciousness, altered states of mind, and collective behaviour. Long-term meditation and spiritual practices can also be studied to see how they affect mental health, emotional well-being, and the growth of human consciousness. This is especially important for learning about the mind-body connection and what it means for mental health.

In the field of sociology, the Maha Kumbh provides

opportunities to study complex social dynamics, group behaviours, cultural exchanges, and the evolution of traditions. This includes how large groups of people interact; how social hierarchies and customs evolve; and how belief systems and cultural practices influence human behaviour on a large scale.

Public health research can use the Maha Kumbh to study the patterns of infectious disease spread within large populations and also gain a better understanding of public health challenges during large public gatherings. This also includes studying sanitation, hygiene, and the effective delivery of health services in challenging environments.

Environmental science can use the Kumbh as a location for understanding the environmental impact of large human gatherings, including the sustainability of practices and conservation strategies. This includes assessing water quality, waste management, energy usage, and the ecological effects of the Kumbh.

Using a unique view of how people are connected, physics can also look into the more subtle aspects of the Maha Kumbh, such as the role of consciousness, human intention, and the relationship between a person and their environment.

The potential in all of these areas is vast and provides an opportunity to expand our understanding of human life and its interactions.

2. Exploring areas like crowd dynamics, mass behaviours, consciousness studies, environmental impacts, and more

The Maha Kumbh, due to its immense scale and complexity, offers extraordinary opportunities for exploring areas of study that are difficult to replicate in laboratory settings. These areas of study each present a valuable area of investigation that can uniquely inform the understanding of the human condition.

The study of crowd dynamics offers an opportunity to explore how large masses of people move, interact, and communicate with one another. This includes studying human flow, social interactions, and the emergence of patterns within the crowd, which is of immense importance for understanding crowd management and planning for large public gatherings.

The study of mass behaviour provides a unique opportunity to study the psychological underpinnings of collective action, including how ideas spread, social norms form, and how collective emotions shape individual behaviors—all of which are important for understanding human social dynamics.

Consciousness studies are also a valuable contribution, providing an opportunity to study the effects of spiritual practices on altered states of mind and the nature of human experience. This includes research into the long-term effects of meditation, contemplation, and other forms of spiritual discipline on consciousness and well-being.

Also, the study of environmental impacts at the Kumbh provides an understanding of the human impact on the local ecosystem. This helps us understand the effect of waste, pollution, and the depletion of natural resources, which ultimately can assist us in implementing sustainable practices.

Other areas that can be explored include the study of human emotions within large-scale events, the study of cross-cultural interactions, and the study of the interrelationship of mind, body, and environment. All of these areas contribute to our understanding of the human condition.

The Maha Kumbh serves as a living laboratory for scientific exploration, and its unique attributes provide an amazing research environment.

3. Potential studies based on the impact of spiritual practices and mental health during Kumbh

The Maha Kumbh provides a unique setting to examine the impacts of spiritual practices and the mental health of individuals involved in this large-scale spiritual gathering. The potential studies in these areas offer opportunities to explore human potential and mental well-being. The impact of spiritual practices is a crucial area of study, and the Maha Kumbh provides a unique opportunity to study the effects of prolonged meditation, yoga, and other forms of spiritual discipline, providing a window into the long-term effects of these practices on the mind, body, and spirit. This includes studying the impact on the neurophysiology, mental states, and overall well-being of individuals, which can help us understand the human potential for positive transformation.

Also, studying mental health during the Kumbh is important because it lets us look into the psychological stress and pressures that people may be facing while being a part of such a large gathering. Their support systems, ways of coping, and ability to maintain mental stability in such a stressful setting can be examined.

Furthermore, research in this area can help in identifying ways to promote positive coping mechanisms and mental resilience, as well as addressing any challenges that may arise. This knowledge has value beyond the Maha Kumbh and can be used to improve mental health in our communities.

The interplay of spiritual practice and mental health provides a rich opportunity for scientific exploration and to better understand and improve the human experience.

4. The unique potential for transdisciplinary studies

The Maha Kumbh, with its complex convergence of multiple factors, is a compelling example of why transdisciplinary studies are so important for understanding complex phenomena.

The unique nature of Maha Kumbh calls for researchers from a broad range of fields to come together and work collaboratively, sharing expertise and insights that would be impossible to find in a single discipline. This transdisciplinary approach helps to create a holistic perspective on complex problems, and it allows for the possibility of insights that may have remained hidden within a traditional scientific approach. By integrating the methodologies of diverse fields, a better understanding of human life in all its complexity may be achieved.

For example, psychologists, sociologists, anthropologists, environmental scientists, and physicists can collaborate to study the multiple aspects of the Kumbh, each contributing their unique areas of expertise. This level of collaboration allows for a richer and more nuanced understanding of the phenomena that are observed at the Maha Kumbh.

Also, researchers can integrate scientific knowledge with cultural and spiritual understanding, gaining a more holistic and interdisciplinary view of the human experience. The Maha Kumbh is a call to action for researchers to collaborate across disciplinary lines, share knowledge, and explore the possibilities of this approach to understanding the human experience.

5. The scientific approach to spiritual practices

The Maha Kumbh presents a unique opportunity to apply scientific methodologies to understand and research spiritual practices. The scientific approach to spiritual practices is not meant to demystify spirituality but to study how these practices operate, what effects they have, and to validate spiritual wisdom through scientific methods. The scientific approach also allows for the integration of qualitative and quantitative methods to give a richer understanding of this unique opportunity.

Through observation, we may study the physiological effects of meditation, yoga, and other practices. This may include brain activity, heart rates, hormonal responses, and other physiological markers, providing insight into the physical aspects of spiritual practice. Similarly, through the collection of quantitative data through surveys and questionnaires, we may study the psychological impact of spiritual practices and how these practices change a person's mental health, emotional well-being, and cognitive functions. The use of qualitative methods will allow researchers to capture the lived experiences, personal stories, and deeper understanding of the participants.

The scientific approach can also be used to investigate the effectiveness of various spiritual practices, with an examination of which ones work best in different contexts. The scientific method provides a framework for ethical investigation, ensuring that research is conducted with respect and that human rights, cultural sensitivities, and the spiritual values of the participants are always considered.

The scientific approach to spiritual practices promotes collaboration across disciplines and traditions, promoting a mutual understanding and respect for the value of both scientific inquiry and spiritual wisdom. The combination of these approaches offers new methods of research that may improve the quality of human life and also create greater understanding and compassion within our world.

CHAPTER 11: THE FUTURE OF SHARED WISDOM

1. The importance of cross-cultural collaborations in research

Cross-cultural collaboration is paramount in unlocking the future potential of the Maha Kumbh as a site for scientific inquiry. Recognising that diverse perspectives and approaches can enrich our understanding of complex phenomena, cross-cultural approaches acknowledge that knowledge is shaped by unique perspectives, values, and traditions. When we approach our research collaboratively with multiple perspectives, we ensure a richer and more comprehensive understanding of the complex human experience.

Cross-cultural collaboration provides a unique approach to scientific study that helps us move beyond the limitations of any single tradition. Also, by working with diverse research teams, we ensure that we are addressing issues that are relevant to our communities and our world. By building teams that include researchers from diverse backgrounds, we ensure that multiple perspectives are incorporated, which promotes more inclusive and relevant research and allows for scientific advancement to benefit all of humanity.

Cross-cultural collaborations promote a deeper level of ethical responsibility, requiring that research be conducted with respect and recognition of cultural practices, which is an essential aspect of working in diverse communities. The Maha Kumbh is not a cultural artefact; it is a vibrant centre of human experience. Understanding it requires a commitment to respect and responsibility. These collaborations build bridges between nations, people, and perspectives by recognising our shared humanity, which is particularly valuable when exploring challenging subjects or topics with a deeply spiritual component.

Cross-cultural collaborations are not only an ethical imperative; they are also critical for advancing the future of research, knowledge, and wisdom.

2. Integrating the wisdom of the Maha Kumbh with contemporary scientific knowledge

Integrating the wisdom of the Maha Kumbh with contemporary scientific knowledge is essential for creating a more holistic and comprehensive understanding of the human condition. This integration offers a unique opportunity to bridge the gap between ancient spiritual insights and modern scientific discoveries, allowing the two areas to inform and expand on each other.

For thousands of years, the Maha Kumbh's wisdom traditions have given people new ideas about consciousness, human potential, and how everything is connected. These new ideas can be very helpful when thinking about scientific exploration because they give us a new way to understand human experience.

In the same way, science gives us strict ways to test and confirm what we already know to be true. It also gives us a way to confirm spiritual wisdom through direct observation, so that scientific knowledge can add to spiritual insights and spiritual wisdom can give context to scientific findings. This also helps to emphasise that there are multiple pathways to truth and that both scientific inquiry and spiritual exploration are valid ways to approach our understanding of the nature of reality. This integration of modern science with the wisdom of ancient cultures also helps us preserve and highlight the knowledge that has evolved through various spiritual traditions and ensures that these insights are available for future generations.

By merging the two areas, we expand the range of possibilities, and we expand the scope of our collective understanding. The integration of these areas allows us to build new frameworks for understanding that are both meaningful and practical, leading to a more comprehensive and useful understanding of the world and ourselves.

3. The value of spiritual and scientific wisdom

Both spiritual and scientific wisdom hold immense value in the exploration of the human experience, offering unique, yet complementary, pathways to understanding our world and ourselves. Recognising that these are both necessary components of understanding provides a framework for a more balanced and comprehensive approach to exploring the human journey.

Spiritual wisdom is deeply rooted in centuries of tradition, contemplation, and practice, providing important insights into human consciousness, purpose, and the interconnectedness of all living beings, offering valuable perspectives on the nature of mind, emotions, and the human experience.

Science also provides unique value by using observation, experimentation, and rigorous testing. This allows us to understand the material world, human physiology, and the physical dimensions of our existence. Science provides a framework for verifying what is known to be true and also for expanding the boundaries of that knowledge.

By combining spiritual and scientific wisdom, we can create

a synergy that may lead to deeper understanding. By integrating these two approaches, we may better comprehend our human experience in all of its complexity. The integration of the two approaches may help us to bridge the gap between faith and reason, providing a more complete picture of reality. The goal is not to see either approach as superior but to see them as complementary.

The combination of spiritual wisdom and scientific understanding ultimately provides us with a more holistic perspective and understanding of humanity.

4. The responsibility of scientists to share their findings and insights

Scientists who engage with the Maha Kumbh bear the ethical responsibility to share their findings and insights with a broader audience. This ethical obligation recognises that scientific knowledge is not just for the scientific community but also for all of humanity, and making this information available is a crucial part of the scientific process.

Scientists must strive to communicate their research in a manner that is accessible to all, avoiding technical jargon and focusing on the implications of their findings for the greater good. This process ensures that the benefits of research extend beyond the scientific community and helps to engage the public.

The sharing of scientific information must be transparent, acknowledging the limitations of research as well as the potential for future exploration. By being open about the research process, we ensure that we are always growing and changing.

Ethical guidelines also call for respect for the cultural sensitivities and human rights of the individuals involved in the research. This means respecting the purpose of the Maha Kumbh, acknowledging that it is primarily a spiritual event and not a scientific laboratory.

Sharing these findings is also an opportunity to promote social change, improve public policy, and work towards creating a more just and equitable world. Therefore, scientists who participate in the Maha Kumbh must conduct research and share their findings to solve humanity's problems.

5. The long-term potential of these collaborations

The long-term potential for scientific collaborations at the Maha Kumbh is immense, offering a pathway to create lasting change, generate valuable insights, and transform the understanding of the human experience. We may unlock possibilities far beyond our current understanding by fostering ongoing partnerships between researchers, communities, and spiritual traditions. This long-term collaboration underscores the significance of the Maha Kumbh as a continuous site of exploration.

Ongoing collaborations can allow for in-depth studies that unfold over many years, leading to a more complete view of the complexities of human life. This is a valuable opportunity to create a holistic approach that looks at research, practice, and long-term impacts, leading to lasting transformations.

Long-term collaborations also provide a valuable opportunity for the development of ethical and responsible research practices, building a more inclusive, ethical, and compassionate approach to research. The benefits of these collaborations are immense, including the advancement of knowledge, the development of practical applications, and the creation of a more just and sustainable world. The long-term potential of the Maha Kumbh is limited only by our vision and our willingness to collaborate and create a better future.

CHAPTER 12: CONCLUSION AND SUGGESTIONS: THE MAHA KUMBH AS A MODEL FOR THE FUTURE AND FURTHER EXPLORATION

1. **conclusion**

1. **Summarising the key findings and insights of the book**

The concluding chapter is dedicated to summarising the key findings and insights that have been discussed throughout the book and providing a clear and concise recap of the main themes and arguments. The summary acts as a reminder of the most important points discussed throughout this study and highlights the main themes that have evolved. The study sheds light on the unique qualities of the Maha Kumbh as a powerful meeting point of spirituality, human experience, and scientific inquiry. It shows how these different areas are linked and can learn from each other. It is highlighted how the Maha Kumbh can be viewed as a living laboratory, offering unique opportunities for scientific research and exploring the significance of the convergence at Prayagraj and the diversity of spiritual and scientific wisdom that has come from India. It also highlights the need for cross-cultural collaborations and shared ethical responsibility in the research. This concluding section also provides the opportunity to synthesise the various points and to allow the reader a comprehensive understanding of all of the major ideas of the study. We design this summary to reinforce the book's overall message and serve as a valuable tool for future consideration and exploration.

2. Reiterating the Maha Kumbh's value as a model for collaborative inquiry

This concluding chapter reinforces the central argument of the book: the Maha Kumbh provides a model for future collaborative inquiry. This reaffirms the unique nature of this event as a dynamic ecosystem that is both scientifically and spiritually valuable and highlights the importance of collaborative research as a tool for exploring complex problems. The Maha Kumbh demonstrates the immense potential of merging scientific inquiry with spiritual traditions, thereby fostering a bridge between scientific study and human experience. This model highlights the importance of diverse approaches to understanding and the integration of multiple perspectives as a key element for future progress. Also, it demonstrates the power of working together and challenges the traditional scientific mindset by creating a framework that is applicable to a wide variety of human endeavours. The value of this model is to show that collaboration is essential for both scientific advancement and for creating a more equitable and just world, and that by working together, we can more effectively approach the complex issues that are present today. The Maha Kumbh offers a path to create a more comprehensive, inclusive, and transformative future.

3. Highlighting the importance of integrating science and spirituality

The chapter stresses the importance of integrating science

and spirituality as complementary paths to understanding the human condition, suggesting that both approaches are valuable for understanding the world and ourselves. The integration of the two approaches challenges the traditional view that they are inherently separate. By merging the two approaches, we seek to bring meaning, value, and purpose to our scientific research. The integration of these areas also enriches the spiritual path with a more solid and scientific understanding of the human experience. There is a call to action to transcend the traditional dichotomy between science and spirit, and to embrace their mutual benefits. They create pathways towards a more just and equitable world. The integration of science and spirituality is not merely a theoretical exercise; it is a practical call for a more complete and harmonious way of living, where both intellect and intuition are valued.

4. The final message is that the Maha Kumbh serves as a source of inspiration for generations

The final message of this book is that the Maha Kumbh serves as a profound source of inspiration for generations to come. This calls to action for continued exploration and reflection that is based on the insights gained from the Maha Kumbh. The Maha Kumbh is a model of human diversity, spiritual seeking, and collaborative effort, demonstrating that large numbers of people may unite with a shared intention of exploration and growth. By reflecting on the unique nature of the Maha Kumbh, we may gain inspiration for new approaches to scientific investigation and the study of human potential. The Maha Kumbh is a reminder that the human journey is one of ongoing discovery, exploration, and understanding. It serves as a guide for future generations to engage in similar endeavours, promoting a continuing interest in human life, awareness, and compassion. The unique power of the Maha Kumbh lies not only in its past but also in its potential for future generations. The Maha Kumbh is a powerful reminder of the transformative possibilities that exist when we embrace diversity, seek truth, and work together.

2. Suggestions:

As discussed in the foregoing sections, the Kumbh Mela, one of the world's largest religious gatherings, offers a rich tapestry of cultural, spiritual, and logistical elements that present numerous avenues for scientific research. Building upon existing studies, potential areas for further exploration include:

1. Astronomical and Astrological Foundations:

Celestial Alignments: Investigate the specific roles of the Sun, Moon, and Jupiter in determining the timing of the Kumbh Mela and analysing their historical and cultural significance within Hindu traditions.

2. Water Quality and Purification Strategies:

Real-Time Monitoring: Assess the effectiveness of real-time water quality monitoring systems in detecting contaminants during the festival.

Advanced Treatment Technologies: Look at new ways to clean water, like the Hybrid Granular Sequencing Batch Reactor (HGSBR) and bioremediation methods, to make sure that the water is safe for everyone.

3. Crowd Management and Sanitation Measures:

Technological interventions: examine the deployment of AI-powered surveillance, integrated command and control centres (ICCC), strategic zoning, and RFID tagging to manage large crowds and ensure safety.

Sanitation Infrastructure: Analyse the adequacy and efficiency of sanitation facilities, waste disposal methods, and hygiene promotion campaigns implemented during the event.

4. Health and Hygiene Practices:

Preventive Healthcare: Investigate the scope and impact of vaccination campaigns and the availability of essential medications to prevent disease outbreaks among pilgrims.

Nutritional Safety: Assess protocols ensuring the safety of food and water provided during the festival, identifying potential contamination risks.

Emergency Preparedness: Evaluate health monitoring systems and emergency response plans designed to manage potential health crises during the mass gathering.

Traditional Health Practices: Explore the role of traditional practices, such as fasting and meditation, in promoting health and well-being among attendees.

5. Environmental Impact and Mitigation Efforts:

Sustainable Practices: Study the implementation of eco-friendly measures, including the use of biodegradable materials and plastic waste reduction initiatives.

Resource Management: Analyse strategies for waste management, water conservation, renewable energy utilisation, and afforestation efforts aimed at minimising the environmental footprint of the festival.

6. Spiritual and Psychological Dimensions:

Mental Health Benefits: Research the psychological effects of participating in the Kumbh Mela, focusing on aspects such as stress reduction, enhanced mental well-being, and the sense of community fostered among attendees.

Spiritual Engagement: Study the impact of devotional activities, including yoga, meditation, prayer, and the recitation of Vedas and Bhajans, on participants' spiritual experiences.

Community Support Systems: Explore how the Kumbh Mela promotes a holistic lifestyle and provides social support, contributing to a sense of purpose and meaning among attendees.

Finally, by delving into these areas, researchers can gain a comprehensive understanding of the intricate interplay between tradition and modernity that defines the Kumbh Mela, highlighting its significance as a marvel of both faith and science.

3. Key Areas for Further Research and Exploration

Potential Areas for Multidisciplinary and Interdisciplinary Research on the Science Behind the Maha Kumbh Mela

The Maha Kumbh Mela is not only a religious and cultural

phenomenon but also a vast field for scientific exploration. Research in various disciplines can offer insights into crowd management, environmental sustainability, health and hygiene, and technological innovations. The Kumbh Mela, one of the world's largest religious gatherings, offers a rich tapestry of cultural, spiritual, and logistical elements that present numerous avenues for scientific research. Building upon existing studies, potential areas for further research and exploration include:

1. Historical and Cultural Significance

Astronomical and Astrological Foundations:

- ➢ Examine celestial alignments and the roles of the Sun, Moon, and Jupiter in determining the festival's timing, along with their religious significance.
- ➢ Explore Jupiter's influence and the astrological beliefs associated with its transit, highlighting its connection to the spiritual sanctity of the Kumbh Mela.

Ancient Astronomical Calculations:

- ➢ Investigate how traditional Hindu astronomical methods determined the timing of the Kumbh Mela.
- ➢ Analyse historical texts and astrological treatises to understand the significance of planetary movements in the festival's schedule.

Impact on Indian Society:

- ➢ Study how the Kumbh Mela has shaped socio-political, economic, and religious structures over centuries.
- ➢ Examine its influence on trade, pilgrimage economies, and societal interactions over different historical periods.

Mythology vs. Scientific Reality:

- ➢ Compare mythological narratives with historical evidence to understand the festival's origins.
- ➢ Investigate the transformation of myths into cultural practices and their impact on contemporary belief systems.

Spiritual and Psychological Dimensions:

- ➢ Research the psychological effects of participating in the

Kumbh Mela, focusing on stress reduction, mental well-being, and the sense of community among attendees.

- ➢ Study the impact of devotional activities, such as yoga, meditation, prayer, and the recitation of Vedas and Bhajans, on participants' spiritual experiences.
- ➢ Explore how the Kumbh Mela promotes a holistic lifestyle and provides social support, contributing to a sense of purpose and meaning among attendees.

2. Water Quality and Purification Strategies

Monitoring Water Quality:

- ➢ Assess the effectiveness of real-time water quality monitoring systems in detecting contaminants during the festival.
- ➢ Study microbial contamination levels before, during, and after the Kumbh Mela to evaluate the impact of mass bathing rituals.

Advanced Treatment Technologies:

- ➢ Look at new ways to clean water, like the Hybrid Granular Sequencing Batch Reactor (HGSBR) and bioremediation methods to make sure that participants always have access to safe water.
- ➢ Analyse the effectiveness of geotube technology and other filtration systems for treating wastewater generated during the event.

3. Advanced Crowd Management Strategies

AI-Powered Surveillance Systems:

- ➢ Examine the effectiveness of artificial intelligence in monitoring and predicting crowd movements to prevent stampedes.

Integrated Command and Control Centre (ICCC):

- ➢ Assess how real-time data analytics improve decision-making for crowd control.

Strategic Zoning for Large Gatherings:

- ➢ Evaluate how predefined zones impact the safety and movement of pilgrims in high-density areas.

RFID-Based Tracking and Safety:

- ➢ Investigate how RFID tagging helps in tracking lost individuals and improving overall security.

4. Sanitation and Waste Management Techniques

Impact of Large-Scale Sanitation Measures:

- ➢ Study how sanitation infrastructure copes with millions of visitors and ways to improve efficiency.

Effectiveness of Temporary Sewage Treatment Plants (STPs):

- ➢ Analyse how temporary STPs process waste and their impact on river pollution.

Innovative Waste Management Solutions:

- ➢ Explore new biodegradable and sustainable waste disposal techniques to reduce environmental impact.

5. Health and Hygiene Innovations

Public Health Risks and Preventive Measures:

- ➢ Research patterns of disease transmission and how public health interventions can reduce risks.

Role of Vaccination in Large Gatherings:

- ➢ Study the effectiveness of vaccination campaigns in preventing the spread of contagious diseases.

Food and Water Safety Mechanisms:

- ➢ Analyse contamination risks in food and water distribution systems and methods for ensuring hygiene.

Health Monitoring and Emergency Response:

- ➢ Investigate how mobile health clinics and telemedicine improve medical response during the event.

Astrological Remedies and Psychological Impact:

- ➢ Explore how faith-based healing practices influence mental and physical health.

6. Environmental Sustainability and Mitigation Efforts

Eco-Friendly Infrastructure and Construction:

- ➢ Study the use of biodegradable materials and sustainable architecture in temporary structures.

Waste Reduction and Recycling Innovations:

- ➢ Evaluate the effectiveness of recycling programs and composting methods in waste management.

Water Conservation and Purification Techniques:

- ➢ Analyse how large-scale water filtration and purification methods help maintain river health.

Integration of Renewable Energy Sources:

- ➢ Assess the feasibility of solar-powered lighting and biofuel alternatives in large-scale events.

Afforestation and Carbon Offset Initiatives:

- ➢ Investigate tree-planting campaigns to counteract carbon emissions and environmental damage.

Location-Specific Environmental Challenges:

- ➢ Compare the ecological impact of the Kumbh Mela across different locations (Prayagraj, Haridwar, Ujjain, Nashik).

7. Other areas

- ➢ Study the infrastructural needs and development in relation to shelter, transport, logistics, etc.
- ➢ All other relevant areas which may need further investigation and development.

Conclusion

By delving into these areas, researchers can gain a comprehensive understanding of the intricate interplay between tradition and modernity that defines the Kumbh Mela. This research highlights the Maha Kumbh Mela as a marvel of both faith and science, offering insights that can enhance public safety, environmental sustainability, and event management.

The festival serves as a vast research laboratory where ancient traditions intersect with modern scientific inquiry, making it a valuable model for future large-scale human gatherings.

BOOKS BY THIS AUTHOR

Mystics Of The Maha Kumbh (Prayag Raj Purna Kumbh Mela)

The book 'Mystics of the Maha Kumbh' (Prayag Raj Purna Kumbh Mela) immerses readers in a global religious gathering. It discusses the Maha Kumbh's shifting surroundings, religious ceremonies, and profound spiritual practices. The book primarily tells the personal experiences of devotees, saints, and seekers who gather to celebrate faith and dedication. The plot revolves around Akharas, which are medieval monastic societies, and the enigmatic Naga Sadhus, who abandon their everyday lives to become spiritually aware. It also addresses lesser-known spiritual gurus whose expertise and simplicity have a significant impact on those looking for spiritual awakening.

The book goes into esoteric practices, meditation techniques, and lessons that can transform your life. It demonstrates how critical it is to preserve India's rich spiritual tradition and apply its timeless principles in contemporary life.

'Mystics of the Maha Kumbh' investigates those who spend their entire lives attempting to solve life's riddles. It honors religion's strength and the universal longing for self-realization. We aim to motivate readers by imparting the wisdom and enchantment of this unique occasion.

Where Can You Find Salvation? Who Will Bless You With Salvation When Your Life Journey Ends? (Kasi, The Moksha Nagari)

The book 'Where Can You Find Salvation? Who will grant you with salvation at the end of your life's journey?' 'Kasi, the Moksha Nagari,' serves as a spiritual guide for both followers of Lord Siva and those seeking liberation (Mukti) and salvation in the holy city of Kasi. Kasi, recognized as one of the world's holiest cities, has unparalleled spiritual significance as a manifestation of the deity Lord Siva. The divine Ganga flowing through its heart purifies everyone who visits Kasi and its banks. People claim to locate Kasi on Lord Siva's trident and to radiate eternal happiness. Kasi's purity surpasses humanity, bringing salvation to all living beings, including humans, animals, birds, and insects. Every breath you take in Kasi is sacred, every sound is holy, and each step brings us closer to moksha (salvation) from the never-ending cycle of birth, death, and rebirth in Samsara. Kasi is more than just a destination for pilgrims and spiritual seekers. People widely recognize Kasi as the city of salvation. Kasi provides a spiritual haven where dedication and heavenly grace come together to guide every soul to liberty from samsara.

Philosophical Teachings & Commandments Of Lord Dattatreya (Shri Kshetra Ganagapur)

The book 'Philosophical Teachings and Commandments of Lord Dattatreya,' (Shri Kshetra Ganagapur) dives deeply into Lord Dattatreya's timeless wisdom, which represents the Trimurti of Brahma, Vishnu, and Shiva. Lord Dattatreya, the eternal teacher, guides seekers to enlightenment with lectures on simplicity, self-realization, and harmonious living, with a focus on the famous pilgrimage destination of Shri Kshetra Ganagapur. The book delves deeply into his philosophical beliefs on Advaita Vedanta (non-dualism), detachment, and the synthesis of knowledge, devotion, and action, encouraging readers to seek inner peace, discipline, and spiritual fulfillment. Lord Dattatreya emphasizes the interconnectivity of creation by drawing lessons from 24

Gurus, including natural components and sentient beings. He highlights the connection between the individual soul (Atman) and the Supreme Consciousness (Brahman), emphasizing the significance of conquering ego and duality in order to obtain liberation.

Dattatreya's teachings emphasize wisdom, compassion, universal brotherhood, and cosmic order, laying the groundwork for spiritual growth. Rituals, festivals, and sacred monuments enhance devotees' faiths at Shri Kshetra Ganagapur, a transforming sanctuary of healing and spiritual energy. Lord Dattatreya's ageless teachings provide practical guidance for overcoming challenges, improving self-awareness, and nurturing inner peace. This comprehensive spiritual handbook encourages simplicity, compassion, and a deep connection to the divine.

ABOUT THE AUTHOR

Dr. C S Rayudu

Dr C.S. Rayudu is an accomplished educator, writer, and spiritual seeker with a strong interest in Indian religion, culture, and ethics. In this book, Dr Rayudu, a lifetime student of India's spiritual legacy, offers a unique perspective that bridges the gap between ancient knowledge and modern scientific understanding.

Dr Rayudu, who previously explored the spiritual landscape of the Maha Kumbh in his book "Mystics of the Maha Kumbh," now focuses on the festival's scientific possibilities. Personal experiences and conversations with spiritual leaders influence his comprehensive research, providing a solid foundation for understanding the intricate interplay of ritual, community, and environment. The book "Maha Kumbh: A Scientific Treasure Trove" demonstrates his dedication to both maintaining India's spiritual history and investigating its significance in a scientific context, making a persuasive case for the integration of these two critical views.

ACKNOWLEDGEMENT

Without the kind support and efforts of many individuals and institutions, we could not have published this book, "Maha Kumbh: A Scientific Treasure Trove." First and foremost, I want to thank the innumerable pilgrims, local communities, and spiritual leaders who shared their time, insights, and experiences with me during the Maha Kumbh, helping me to gain a better appreciation of this incredible event.

I am very grateful to Gurus for their tremendous advice, mentorship, and continuous support throughout this study project. They provided essential feedback on earlier drafts and crucial ideas that profoundly influenced the final product.

I am also appreciative to the online contributors for providing access to their materials and assisting me in browsing the collection.

Finally, I'd like to thank my family members: my wife, C. Subhasini; my daughter, C. Sushma; and my boys, Sugun and Susheel, for their patience, encouragement, and steadfast support for this effort. Your understanding and kindness were critical in finishing this work.

www.ingramcontent.com/pod-product-compliance
Ingram Content Group UK Ltd.
Pitfield, Milton Keynes, MK11 3LW, UK
UKHW021408190726
13845UKWH00028B/947

9 789334 213140